LIVING AND PRAYING
IN JESUS' NAME

Living & Praying

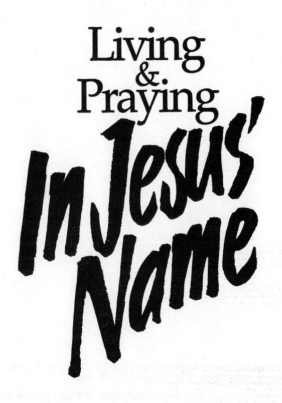

In Jesus' Name

Dick Eastman
&
Jack Hayford

Tyndale House
Publishers, Inc.
Wheaton, Illinois

For information on training materials from Dick Eastman write: Change the World Ministries, P.O. Box 5838, Mission Hills, CA 91345.

For information on the training materials available from Jack Hayford write: Living Way Ministries, 14344 Sherman Way, Van Nuys, CA 91405.

The authors wish to gratefully acknowledge several primary sources of reference that were especially helpful in the preparation of this book. We also wish to express our gratitude for the kind permission of the publishers to quote freely from the pages of these resources: From *The Search for God*, by David Manning White, copyright 1983. Reprinted by permission of Macmillan Publishing Company. From *Eerdman's Book of Famous Prayers*, Veronica Zundel, copyright 1983. Reprinted by permission of Wm. B. Eerdmans Publishing Company. From *All the Divine Names and Titles in the Bible*, by Herbert Lockyer, copyright 1975. Reprinted by permission of the Zondervan Company.

All Scripture quotations are from *The Holy Bible*, New King James Version (NKJV), copyright 1982 by Thomas Nelson, Inc., unless otherwise noted as being from *The Living Bible (TLB)*, copyright 1971 by Tyndale House Publishers or from *The Holy Bible*, New International Version (NIV), copyright 1978, 1984 by the New York International Bible Society.

Library of Congress Catalog Card Number 88-71952
ISBN 0-8423-2667-7
Printed in the United States of America

4   5   6   7   8   9   10   11   94   93   92   91   90   89

To him
Who sits on the throne
And to the Lamb
Be praise and honor
And glory and power,
For ever and ever!
(Revelation 5:13, NIV)

Write your blessed
name, O Lord, upon
my heart, there to
remain so indelibly
engraved, that no
prosperity, no
adversity shall ever
move me from your
love. Be to me a
strong tower of
defense, a comforter
in tribulation, a
deliverer in distress,
a very present help
in trouble, and a
guide to heaven
through the many
temptations and
dangers of this life.
(Thomas à Kempis)

CONTENTS

INTRODUCTION

IN HIS NAME

A friend asked Mrs. Albert Einstein if she understood the theory of relativity. "No, not at all," she answered. Then she added with a chuckle, "But I understand Albert, and he can be trusted!"

It's doubtful any phrase in our prayer vocabulary is voiced more frequently, or understood less, than the three-word expression "in Jesus' name."

Yet our capacity to trust the Lord is clearly linked in Scripture to our knowledge of His name. The psalmist said, "Those who know Your name will put their trust in You!" (Ps. 9:10). Victory in battle is likewise linked to the power of His name: "Through You we will push down our enemies; through Your name we will trample those who rise up against us" (Ps. 44:4-5).

Later Christ extended to His disciples a certain "power of attorney"—the authority to use His name in transacting business on His behalf. He said, "And whatever You ask in My name, that I will do, that the Father may be glorified in the Son" (John 14:13).

But how do we apply all this in practical terms as we endeavor to live and pray today "in Jesus' name"? The author of Proverbs hints at an answer when he declares, "The name of the Lord is a strong tower; the righteous run to it and are safe" (Prov. 18:10).

Living and praying in Jesus' name means much more than merely voicing a three-word expression at the end of a prayer. It is to *move into* Jesus' name through prayer; it is to step into each new day in the power of who Jesus is.

Living and praying in Jesus' name begins by our pursuing a disciplined awareness of His nature and character as revealed by the many names and titles He is assigned in Scripture. Then it continues when we saturate ourselves, even systematically, with an understanding of what it means to live and pray in the power of a specific facet of Christ's person.

As we pursue this study, keep in mind the simple dictionary definition of *name:* "A word or words by which an entity is designated and distinguished from others." Andrew Murray amplifies this thought:

> What is a person's name? It is a word or expression in which a person is represented to us. When I mention or hear a name, it brings to mind the whole man, what I know of him, and also the impression he has made on me. The name of a king includes his honor, his power, his kingdom. His name is the symbol of his power. And so each name of God embodies and represents some part of the glory of the Unseen One. The name of Christ is the expression of everything he has done and everything he is and lives to do as our Mediator.[1]

Every name and title on the pages following applies specifically and directly to our Lord Jesus Christ. True, some descriptions are of Old Testament origin and might be labeled "titles of God," but keep in mind that according to the New Testament, all the fullness of the Godhead dwells bodily in Christ's person (Col. 2:9). Paul also wrote, "God was in Christ reconciling the world to Himself . . ." (2 Cor. 5:19), while John said, "The Word (Christ) was God" and "The Word (Christ/God) became flesh" (John 1:1, 14). Thus, all that we might say of God also applies to Christ. The fullness of the Father flows out to us in His Son: "He who has seen Me has seen the Father" (John 14:9). There is neither competition between nor confusion among the Godhead. The Father is pleased to have all fullness dwell in Christ, and the Holy Spirit delights to exalt Him fully (Col. 1:19; John 16:14).

Finally, to assist you in your systematic pursuit of this potentially life-changing quest, we've selected thirty-one examples of these titles of Christ, one for each day of the month. You will also notice we've begun each chapter with a primary "focus" word for each theme. We hope this will help you understand the principal of a specific title. With each name or title you'll also find a list of related expressions, some more extensive than others, to help you "hallow" (or sanctify) Jesus' name more specifically. In this way you will apply that portion of the Lord's Prayer: "Hallowed be Your name" (Matt. 6:9).

So, beloved, bathe yourself today in the cleansing freshness of a knowledge of Christ's name. Our prayer for you is that in this time of freshness you will find fulfillment in God's promise: "I will set him on high, because he has known My name!" (Ps. 91:14).

A WALL OF FIRE
Zechariah 2:5

PROTECTION

A unique picture of God's protective providence emerged nearly a hundred years ago during the formative years of the China Inland Mission. It was reported that a young missionary to China felt called to take the gospel to a much-neglected region of China's interior. That neglect, however, was not due to a lack of vision so much as to the hostile nature of the inhabitants of the region. Portions of the primary road leading to the region were plagued by gangs of ruthless bandits. Still, the missionary had a burden to evangelize the people of the region, and so—against the advice of his colleagues—he set out to do so.

After making the journey, during which he traveled the troubled road preaching joyfully and without incident, he returned to his base untouched. Naturally, fellow workers wondered how he was able to accomplish his objective without even once seeing the bandits. After all, it was impossible for a foreigner to travel through the region without the "locals" knowing of it.

Soon a rumor began circulating throughout the province, and it appeared to have been started by the bandits themselves. According to the rumor, this particular missionary escaped attack because he was the only foreigner to visit that region accompanied by a personal entourage of soldiers. The rumor even placed the number of soldiers at precisely eleven.

The missionary was stunned, as were his colleagues, for clearly he had made the trip alone. Had angels come into the conflict on his behalf? He was sure they had, but why eleven? His answer came later in response to a letter he sent detailing the miracle to his sponsoring church back home.

Some weeks after the missionary sent his letter he received a note from his pastor inquiring if he could recall the exact date he first entered the hostile area. The missionary knew the precise date and quickly responded.

After more than a month, a most amazing letter arrived from the missionary's pastor. The minister explained that several days prior to the date the missionary started his journey, he had been stirred by God to call a special prayer meeting on behalf of this missionary friend. When the appointed day arrived, however, the pastor had been greatly disappointed by the poor attendance. That was, until he received the missionary's unusual testimony. The pastor's letter then concluded, "You'll be pleased to know that, counting myself, there were exactly eleven of us who were praying for you that very day."

KNOWING THIS NAME

Whether the missionary was aware of it or not, he had been functioning within the power of one of Jesus' mighty names, "a Wall of Fire," a title that comes from our Lord Himself through the pen of Zechariah (Zech. 2:5).

The Lord gives us this promise to be a wall of fire, providing protection against our enemies, in a most unusual setting. Zechariah's prophecy follows the return of thousands of Jews after seventy years of Babylonian captivity. The city of Jerusalem to which they returned was in shambles. Not only had the wall been broken down decades earlier by Nebuchadnezzar's troops, but the temple had been completely destroyed.

With zeal and devotion the returned exiles, under Zerubbabel's leadership, set about rebuilding the temple, seeking to reestablish that center for the worship of the Most High God. But the building process was slow, and the zeal of the workers was subject to discouragement and weariness. Critics and oppressive neighbors assailed their efforts and even legal maneuvers were made to hinder them.

Amid all this, the devoted team of builders was always vulnerable to the "sniping" of enemies who took advantage of the fact that they had no wall to protect them. Thus they were seeking to accomplish a successful building project without the conventional protection such an effort usually required. It is at this point that the word of the Lord came to the prophet Zechariah, instructing him to tell Jerusalem that "I (God) will be a wall of fire all around her" (2:5).

Zechariah's announcement became a great reassuring promise. And the evidence of history is not only that Zerubbabel pursued the project of rebuilding the temple until completion, but that the opposition against God's people was completely overthrown. The Lord, indeed, had become their Wall of Fire.

LIVING THIS NAME

In order to understand and apply Jesus' name, our Wall of Fire, we must address two principal questions: To whom is the promise made, and what makes up the wall?

It's true that the ancient promise of Zechariah 2:5 was made to Jerusalem or, more specifically, to her inhabitants. However, it is not a violation of either the letter or the spirit of this passage to apply this promise on a personal level today. The New Testament teaches that all Christians who comprise the church of this age (that is, all who have committed their lives to Christ) have "come to Mt. Zion . . . the heavenly Jerusalem" (Heb. 12:22). Therefore, as citizens of the City of God we are assured of the benefits that come with "dwelling" in this stronghold (see Ps. 48). Thus, if the Lord said, "I will be a wall of fire all around (Jerusalem)," this means He is also a wall of fire about us today.

And note how David extols the security and defensibility of Jerusalem by reason of God's presence dwelling there. He says, "God is in her palaces; He is known as her refuge" (Ps. 48:3). The certainty of protection is based on God's presence as, among other things, a wall of fire. Note again these words from Zechariah 2:5: "'For I,' says the Lord, 'will be a wall of fire all around her, and I will be the glory in her midst.'"

The fire, of course, is the outflowing radiance of the Lord's glory. The brightness and splendor that filled the tabernacle in Moses' time and that flooded the temple when Solomon dedicated it to the Lord is the same *shekinah* glory that God promises will encircle His own and preserve them from the enemy.

15

The wall is the very presence of the Lord's person that rises up to protect His people just as the walls of ancient cities rose up to protect their inhabitants. And this happens for God's people in three unique ways.

First, *our Lord's name, a Wall of Fire, separates.* This separating action of God's "glory fire" is seen in Numbers 16:35. There we discover the dramatic episode of Moses' confrontation with Korah, which is climaxed by God's drawing a line of judgment between the obedient and the rebellious. Note how the fire that "came out from the Lord" (Num. 16:35) clearly depicts God protecting His own while at the same time vindicating Moses and Aaron. And since Jesus taught us to pray, "Deliver us from evil" (Matt. 6:13), we, too, can rest assured that our Lord, a Wall of Fire, will vindicate us. He will defend us from evil that assails us. And He will confront sin in our lives whenever we need His purifying fire.

Second, *our Lord's name, a Wall of Fire, insulates.* The forty-year sojourn of Israel through the wilderness provides a perfect example of this protection. The presence of God, seen as a fiery pillar by night and a covering cloud by day, was not only a sign of His glory but a physical reality that had a beneficial effect. Growing up in a desert climate like southern California one quickly understands the extremes of terribly hot days followed by very cold nights. It is not difficult to imagine how God's people appreciated the cooling effect of the cloud by day followed by the warming effect of the fire at night. As the Scripture declares, "He spread a cloud for a covering, and a fire to give light (and warmth) in the night" (Ps. 105:39). What a joy to know that Jesus' name insulates us against such things as a fiery blast from Satan or the cold chills of spiritual indifference.

Finally, *our Lord's name, a Wall of Fire, terminates.* Praise God for those times when He barricades the enemy's advance against us—not unlike those occasions when a law enforcement team blockades a road to contain and restrain a violent criminal. The blockade (or wall) terminates the advance of that criminal. And notice how the same cloud of "glory fire" which insulated Israel during their wilderness journey also terminated the Egyptian's pursuit at the Red Sea. Exodus 14:19-21 relates how the fiery cloud literally "walled off" Pharaoh's troops, blocking their path with darkness, while at the same time becoming a warm wall of brightness to God's people awaiting their deliverance.

16

So rejoice, beloved, as you contemplate today. No matter what you do or where you go, a Wall of Fire is with you.

PRAYING THIS NAME

Only those who learn to pray in Jesus' name will truly learn to live in the power of His name. That's why it's so important for us to realize that praying in Jesus' name is far more than a mere mentioning of these three words at the end of a prayer. Praying in Jesus' name means we take the reality of God's nature and character as seen in a particular name or title of our Lord and saturate our prayer awareness with it. Further, we must realize that all that God is, Christ is also. All the fullness of God dwells in Him (Col. 2:9). To employ the concept of our Lord as a wall of fire in our prayer is to recognize that, to the evil inhabitants of the unseen realm (demonic forces), Christ indeed represents all that a wall of fire is in the physical realm. Thus, to pray in Jesus' name, a Wall of Fire, is to move into the fiery enclosure of His presence while we're praying.

It is to pray with Catherine of Siena, who sought her Savior, a Wall of Fire, six centuries ago:

> O eternal Godhead, O sea profound, what more could You give me than Yourself? You are the fire that ever burns without being consumed; You consume in Your heat all the soul's self-love; You are the fire which takes away cold; with Your light You illuminate me so that I may know all Your truth. Clothe me, clothe me with Yourself, eternal truth, so that I may run this mortal life with true obedience, and with the light of Your most holy faith.[1]

TODAY'S PRAYER

Today, O Lord,
I come with praise to the gates of Your holy temple
to give thanks for Your promise of protection.
As a wall of fire, dear Savior,
keep me entirely unto Yourself.
I humbly pray, protect me from
wandering from Your commands,
and deliver me from the evil one.

I come within the shielding protection
of Your insulating provision,
Thanking You that the wall which surrounds me
    is a covering as well.
And concerning those points of pursuit
wherein the enemy seeks to gain the advantage
of me, my loved ones, or any of Your own whom I name—
in Jesus' name, my Wall of Fire,
stop the adversary's action and restrain his advances.

My eyes are upon You,
my Lord and my God—
my provision for protection
and my Wall of Fire.
In Jesus' name.
Amen.

HALLOWING THIS NAME

Each chapter will conclude with several suggestions of additional
names and titles of our Lord. You may wish to include these in
your prayers of praise as you "hallow" (sanctify) the name of
Jesus. Following are the names and titles that relate to the image
of the Lord, a Wall of Fire:

Brightness of His Glory—Heb. 1:3
Consuming Fire—Heb. 12:29
Cover from the Tempest—Isa. 32:2
Flame—Isa. 10:17
Hiding Place from the Wind—Isa. 32:2
Jehovah-Nissi (The Lord My Banner)—Exod. 17:15
Jehovah-Shammah (The Lord Is There)—Ezek. 48:35
My High Tower—Ps. 144:2
My Shield—Ps. 115:11
Refiner and Purifier—Mal. 3:3
Refuge from the Storm—Isa. 25:4
Shade—Ps. 121:5
Shadow from the Heat—Isa. 25:4
Shield—Gen. 15:1; Deut. 33:29
Sun and Shield—Ps. 84:11
Wall in Judah—Ezra 19:9

2
A SURE FOUNDATION
Isaiah 28:16

STABILITY

Hollywood, California—many people come there from around the world frantically seeking success, fame, and fortune. For most, however, the quest is a futile one. Only a few have actually "made it" to the sidewalk along Hollywood Boulevard, where embedded bronze symbols bear the names and faces of the famous. It appears that these men and women, in worldly terms, have mastered their destinies. And yet, upon passing this way and looking at these small monuments more carefully, one cannot help but be touched with a sense of irony. The same sidewalk in which the coveted star has been firmly laid is cluttered with debris, splattered with mud, and ground over in places with patches of gum.

In stark contrast, the promise of God to His people says succinctly, "I lay in Zion . . . *a sure foundation*" (Isa. 28:16).

Here we discover another title for our Lord, a title based not on the counsel of man, but based securely in the counsel of God. Life is lifted from the clay of this world's quicksand and established on the rock of God's sure purposes. His Word declares, "I waited patiently for the Lord; and He inclined to me, and heard my cry. He also brought me up out of a horrible pit, out of the miry clay, and set my feet upon a rock, *and* established my steps" (Ps. 40:1-2.)

The reward of walking this "established" path is only found in

God's Word. There is no bronze star waiting to be laid in concrete by the hands of man and tarnished by the passage of time. Rather, as Daniel declared, the redeemed of the Lord—those whose lives are built upon the sure foundation laid by God—shall shine "like the stars forever and forever!" (Dan. 12:3).

KNOWING THIS NAME

But what do we mean when we refer to our Lord as a "sure foundation"? All of Isaiah 28 is a statement concerning God's commitment to introduce stability into a society immersed in uncertainty. It is here that we see the revelation of this name.

The setting of this prophecy is during the reign of Ahaz, one of Judah's most wicked kings. At the height of his apostasy, Ahaz actually shut the door of the temple of the Lord in Jerusalem—he had already emptied it of all its holy objects dedicated for priestly worship. The wickedness of Ahaz invoked a season of suffering upon Judah and defeat was experienced twice: once at the hands of Pekah the Syrian and later during a civil war against the northern kingdom of Israel. This latter defeat resulted in the death of Ahaz's son and the loss of over two hundred thousand of his own people who were taken captive (see 2 Chron. 28).

In this scriptural setting—which describes a people who "err in vision" and "stumble in judgment," and who will ultimately "fall backward, and be broken and snared and caught" (Isa. 28:7, 13)—the prophet issues a contrasting promise. He declares the Lord's commitment to preparing the way for His chosen to rise as a people who will stand solidly and securely amid the sliding uncertainty that characterized the culture of the day. Through Isaiah the Lord declared, "Behold I lay in Zion a stone for a foundation, a tried stone, a precious cornerstone, *a sure foundation* . . ." (Isa. 28:16, italics added). The heart of God's promise through Isaiah is this: No matter how uncertain the world scene may be or how slippery our society is, there is a solid place on which the followers of Jesus can stand. And that place is His name—a Sure Foundation.

The force of this title and the truth it teaches are found in the fact that God Himself pledges to lay this foundation. This is not a task assigned to men or angels. God is the one committing Himself to establish a place where life can be lived with stability and certainty. A tremendous surge of confidence should rise in the heart of a believer who receives this prophetic word. After all, foundations are laid as the base of an edifice, and if God lays a foundation, it is certain that something is going to be built. God is not in the habit of starting projects that are left uncompleted. The Bible says, "He who has begun a good work in you will complete *it* until the day of Jesus Christ" (Phil. 1:6).

The remarkable thing about this foundation, however, is not only the promise it provides for a future development but the stability it provides for a future durability. Note the word *sure*. "I lay . . . a sure foundation." The Hebrew word employed here, *yasad*, was commonly used to describe the establishing of a foundation. But it also was used with reference to rulers or counselors "sitting together" in conference. It suggests that careful consultation will insure stable planning, a truth emphasized by the writer of Proverbs who declares wisdom is secured by a "multitude of counselors" (Prov. 11:14; 15:22).

In this light we can see something of the depth of the footings our Lord is laying, footings upon which we're to build our lives. God hasn't built a hurried foundation, so there's no reason for us to be hurried—especially since hurry often results in instability. Indeed, the prophecy concludes, "Whoever believes will not act hastily."

LIVING THIS NAME

There is something of a frantic quality to the world around us; people grasping for brass rings, stampeding to seize opportunities, rushing to find momentary pleasure. So persistent is this tide of human questing that it is easy to be caught up in it, to become urgent and desperate about living rather than resting in confidence, waiting upon the Lord for the unfolding of His plan. How important it becomes to remember God's pledge: "Behold, I lay in Zion . . . a sure foundation." It seems that God is trying to get our attention, to stop our breakneck pace with the word, *Behold!*

"Look!" He's saying to us, "See what solid ground I have established for building your life and working out its problems; for making your decisions and developing your plans. Look! It's solid ground, sure footing, an established foundation. In My name you will find stability!"

PRAYING THIS NAME

Stability, indeed, is a foundational quality of the name of Jesus. To pray in Jesus' name is to approach His throne with unqualified assurance. It is to pray as Thomas Aquinas did, who confidently petitioned:

> Give me, O Lord, a steadfast heart,
> which no unworthy affection may drag downwards;
> give me an unconquered heart,
> which no tribulation can wear out;
> give me an upright heart,
> which no unworthy purpose may tempt aside.
> Bestow on me also, O Lord my God,
> understanding to know You,
> diligence to seek You,
> wisdom to find You,
> and a faithfulness that may finally embrace You,
> through Jesus Christ our Lord. Amen.[1]

As you offer similar petitions, think of areas in your Christian walk where there is the potential for instability. Consider the immediate hours ahead and ask the Lord to reveal possible danger points. Then claim His name for these circumstances. Declare that His name has gone before you by faith and established stability in that situation even before it happens. Pray as John Wesley did just before embarking on a particularly treacherous mission:

> Fix Thou our steps, O Lord, that we stagger not at the world, but steadily go on to our glorious home; neither censuring our journey by the weather we meet with, or turning out of the way for anything that befalls us.
>
> The winds are often rough, and our own weight presses us downwards. Reach forth, O Lord, Thy hand, Thy saving hand, and speedily deliver us.
>
> Teach us, O Lord, to use this transitory life as pilgrims returning to their beloved home; that we may take what our journey requires, and not think of settling in a foreign country.[2]

TODAY'S PRAYER

Holy Father God,
I come to wait quietly before You.
The spirit of the age would press my pace
beyond the wisdom of waiting.
It would tell me if I don't hurry, I can't get ahead.
But I hear You calling me to quietness as I pray in Jesus' name,
taking my place upon the sure foundation
You have laid for my life in Him.

I come in prayer to affirm this day,
"My hope is built on nothing less!"
Establish my steps today, dear Lord.
Let the fruit of my life be enduring
because my steps are ordered within Your counsels.
In the name of my Sure Foundation I pray—
Jesus,
Your Son,
my Savior.
Amen!

HALLOWING THIS NAME

Covenant of the People—Isa. 42:6
Fortress—Ps. 18:2
Foundation—Isa. 28:16
My Rock of Refuge—Ps. 31:2
My Stay—2 Sam. 22:19; Ps. 18:18
Refuge from the Storm—Isa. 25:4
Rock of My Salvation—2 Sam. 22:7
Sanctuary—Isa. 8:14
Strong Lord—Ps. 89:8 (KJV)
Strong Tower—Ps. 61:3
Stronghold—Nah. 1:7
Surety—Heb. 7:22
That Spiritual Rock—1 Cor. 10:4

3

A REFINER AND PURIFIER
Malachi 3:3

GROWTH

With his head hanging in remorse, five-year-old Johnny made his way to the bathroom to wash his hands. Only minutes earlier the child had staunchly refused to do so, to the point of near rebellion—until Mommy threatened him with a good spanking.

Some moments later Mom happened down the hallway. Through a crack in the bathroom door she overheard Johnny mumbling to himself. Stretching to reach the sink, his hands lathered to the hilt, Johnny declared repeatedly, "Jesus and germs, Jesus and germs. That's all I ever hear around here, and I haven't seen either one of them yet!"

God's goal for every redeemed soul this side of heaven is spiritual purity and growth. He longs to cleanse us of those spiritual "germs" that ultimately would rob us of purity. That's why our faith is sometimes "tried with fire" as Peter suggests (1 Pet. 1:7).

In his *Sermons,* Phillips Brooks explains, "In what strange quarries and stone-yards the stones for the celestial wall are being hewn! Out of the hillsides of humiliated pride; deep in the darkness of crushed despair; in the fretting and dusty atmosphere of little cares; in the hard cruel contacts that man has with man; wherever souls are being tried and ripened, in whatever commonplace and homely ways—there God is hewing out the pillars for His temple."[1]

Indeed, God is ever drawing us closer to the fire of His purifying essence so we might be more like Him. And surely there is much within the nature of us all that needs purifying. As Thomas a' Kempis expressed in *The Imitation of Christ,* "I never found yet any religious person so perfect but that he had sometimes absenting of grace or some diminishing of fervor; and there was never yet any saint so highly rapt but that, first or last, he had some temptation. He is not worthy to have the high gift of contemplation that hath not suffered for God some tribulation."[2]

All, indeed, have sinned and come short of the glory of God (Rom. 3:23). And even after we've surrendered our lives to Christ, there are frequent reminders that each of us is human. Most can identify with the bumper sticker that reads, "Lead me not into temptation. I can find it for myself!" I'm sure all committed Christians would agree: We need a cleansing, purifying agent to help us grow. And in Jesus' name, our Refiner and Purifier, we will find this agent!

KNOWING THIS NAME

It is Malachi who paints a picture of our Lord, a Refiner and Purifier (Mal. 3:3). He gives this description in a prophecy meant to deal with a complaining people who had forgotten God's faithfulness. Over the years a new generation of Israelites had risen, a generation so self-centered and consumed with their own interests that serving the Lord was a point of formalism at best—begrudging participation at worst. The Lord spoke repeatedly through His prophetic messenger Malachi, charging the people to repent, only to have each charge repealed with rebuttal and countercharges.

"It isn't really worth it to serve God," the people seemed to say (Mal. 3:14). When the Lord challenged their indifference regarding His altar of sacrifice (upon which His people had presented defiled offerings), it was as though the self-serving "saints" demanded, "What are You talking about?" (Mal. 1:6).

This scene from the final book of the Old Testament is one of stagnation. It is a scene revealing people who are accustomed to being around godliness, but unwilling to grow up. Yet, amid this picture of a passive people who resist the correction of the Lord, God's promise rings out: "The Lord . . . will suddenly come to His temple!" (Mal. 3:1). He declares that a visitation of His presence is coming, and it will be as purging and purifying as when a refiner works with precious metals. The prophecy proclaims, "He will be like a refiner's fire or a launderer's soap" (Mal. 3:2, NIV). In short, the Lord committed Himself to work with a people who would allow Him to grow them up! And now, as then, He seeks saints who are willing to permit Him to refine their character as well as purify their lives.

LIVING THIS NAME

The two images presented in this title of our Lord, fire and soap, warmly invite our trust and gently urge us to let the Lord have His way in our lives—all day long, not just in the prayer closet. We need to live in the dual reality that Christ is our Refiner and Purifier.

First, *the figure of a launderer's soap brings to mind the everyday process of washing clothes.* We've all watched what happens when we put clothing in the water, add soap, and then start the washer. Given time, the mere presence of the soap will penetrate and cleanse the clothing.

This simple lesson is assuring and encouraging: If we will simply allow the presence of Jesus to invade any point of uncleanness in us, at any time, on any day, He will readily cleanse it. It is not a matter of our reciting holy incantations or attempting religious programs of self-improvement. It is simply a matter of inviting Jesus into the unclean part of our lives. You might feel ashamed to ask Him there, but He who left the excellence of heaven to condescend to the pollution of earth is not threatened by either the presence or power of sin. "He who is in you is greater," the Bible says (1 John 4:4). If your mind, heart, habit, or actions are contradicting God's desire for growth in you, invite Jesus into your failures, into the very point of that uncleanness. He's like a launderer's soap. His presence, like the old soap commercial says, "gets the dirt out, good!"

Second, *the image of a metal refiner in Malachi 3:3 depicts our Lord's gentleness.* The soap works with strength; the refiner works with sensitivity. Metal, even such precious substances as gold and silver, is refined by removing the impurities. This is done by melting the metal. As a result of the melting, the impurities (or "dross") rise to the surface. Then the refiner carefully draws this dross off the top, patiently working until a perfect, mirrorlike quality exists on the surface of the molten metal. If too much temperature is applied, the metal will burn; if too little, all the impurities will not be removed. Thus the finest refiner is the one who sensitively applies just enough heat to complete the task, and who exercises all the patience needed to remove each impurity until the clarity of the surface literally mirrors the image of the refiner.

PRAYING THIS NAME

Although God's purifying power works continuously, it is during prayer that we become quietly conscious of its full reality. Often it is only in prayer that God reveals areas of needed growth. When we pray in Jesus' name, our Refiner and Purifier, we sensitize our awareness to the gentle "searchings" of the Holy Spirit, allowing Him to surface these secret sins during prayer. This kind of praying is similar to Christina Rossetti's prayer a century ago:

> As the wind is Thy symbol, so forward our goings.
> As the dove, so launch us heavenwards.
> As water, so purify our spirits.
> As a cloud, so abate our temptations.
> As dew, so revive our languor.
> As fire, so purge out our dross.[3]

It's true that sometimes in prayer we may feel as though "the heat is on," or that we're sitting on a celestial "hot seat." Yet, as uncomfortable as this may be at the time, we must realize it is simply our Refiner and Purifier at work "growing us up." He's pushing things to the surface that need to be removed, cleansed.

Never be afraid to allow the Lord, through your prayers, to burn away that which hinders His glory from reflecting through you. George Whitefield once visited a glass factory where he observed several masses of burning glass of various forms. The workman would take a piece of glass and put it first into one flame, then into a second flame, and finally he would put the same lump into a third flame. Whitefield asked why it was necessary for the glass to go through so many fires. The craftsman responded, "Well, sir, the first was not hot enough nor was the second; therefore we put it into a third, and that will make it transparent."

So let's petition God today for a new transparency in Jesus' name, our Refiner and Purifier. We might begin by praying with St. Augustine:

> O Lord, the house of my soul is narrow;
> enlarge it, that You may enter in.
> It is ruinous, O repair it!
> It displeases Your sight;
> I confess it, I know.
> But who shall cleanse it, to whom shall I cry out but to You?
> Cleanse me from my secret faults, O Lord,
> and spare Your servant from strange sins.[4]

TODAY'S PRAYER

Lord Jesus Christ,
today I want to live
in the resources of Your personal ministry
as my Refiner and Purifier.

I choose to allow You to grow me up!
Right now, I openly expose those places
   where sin infests my thoughts, my habits, my living.
I not only ask Your forgiveness,
I invite Your presence like cleansing soap.
Launder my soul, my mind—today.

And Lord,
wherever the fire of refinement needs
   to be brought to bear upon my being,
I open to Your gentle ministry.
Remove all dross.
Take out whatever cheapens the treasured quality
of Your eternal workings in me.

And, dear Savior,
don't stop until Your image can be seen.
For I pray this in Your name,
my Refiner and Purifier.
Amen.

HALLOWING THIS NAME

Holy—Isa. 6:3; 57:15
Holy and Reverend—Ps. 111:9
Holy and True—Rev. 6:10
Holy One and the Just—Acts 2:27; 3:14
Holy One of Israel—Isa. 49:7
Jehovah-Mekaddishkem (The Lord Our Sanctifier)—Lev. 20:8
Jesus Christ the Righteous—1 John 2:1
Lamb without Blemish—1 Pet. 1:19
Lord Our Righteousness—Jer. 23:6
Mediator of the New Covenant—Heb. 12:24
Minister of the Sanctuary—Heb. 8:2
Most Holy—Dan. 9:24
Propitiation for Our Sins—1 John 2:2
Ransom—Mark 10:45
Redeemer—Isa. 59:20
Root out of Dry Ground—Isa. 53:2
Tender Grass—2 Sam. 23:4
Vine—John 15:1, 5

4
A NAIL FASTENED IN A SURE PLACE
Isaiah 22:23, KJV

SECURITY

Two persons flying in the same plane during severe turbulence may have vastly different feelings regarding their security. Although both might be equally safe, one may be filled with fear because he fails to understand the qualities of the aircraft and the principles upon which it was constructed. The other person may know that even the severity of the turbulence could not possibly destroy the craft, and so he is unafraid. Because the latter is well acquainted with the principles of the vessel's construction and understands the laws by which the plane is governed, he is secure.

So it is with those who understand the character of Christ and the principles concerning the power of His name. If, for example, we understand those principles regarding our security in Christ—specifically the power of His blood and its superiority over Satan—then we may rest secure with great delight under "the shadow of the Almighty" (Ps. 91:1). If, however, we think we're trusting Christ but our faith is feeble, we will be less secure.

KNOWING THIS NAME

A fuller understanding of the security we have in Jesus' name can be found in examining Isaiah's rather unique description of our Lord as "a nail (fastened) in a sure place" (Isa. 22:23, KJV).

In ancient times it was the custom of victorious kings to bring trophies of war into the temple of the particular gods they worshiped, there to be hung for display on pegs fixed in the temple walls. The reasons for this custom were clear. First, the trophies (or "spoils") were valuable, for they were usually made of precious metals or stone. Second, they were kept as a demonstration of the faithfulness of their supposed "god," who they believed secured for them a victory and thus was worthy of worship at that particular shrine. This custom was not only practiced in the pagan world at the time of our text (Isaiah 22), but in Israel and Judah as well.

In Isaiah's prophecy we find a graphic picture of the coming Messiah using this very image. Here the Messiah is pictured in the person of Eliakim (Isa. 22:20) who was the keeper of the castle during the reign of King Hezekiah (2 Kings 18:18). The dramatic story, as unfolded in 2 Kings 18 and 19, relates the unforgettable incident of Rabshakeh's threat against Jerusalem in the name of Assyria's king, Sennacherib. The account in 2 Kings, joined with Isaiah's words in his prophecy (Isa. 22:15-25), indicates that a controversy had arisen between those upon whom Hezekiah was depending at this crucial time. Apparently Eliakim stood firm in the faith, believing that God's promise of deliverance would be forthcoming, while Shebna, the scribe, was roundly cursed for conceding to unbelief (Isa. 22:15-19). In bright contrast to the scattering and destruction Shebna would suffer, the words of Eliakim foretold what the Messiah would become to His own. Scripture declares, "I will fasten him as a peg in a secure place" (Isa. 22:23, NIV). This is to say, "I will make him as a secure support for every trophy of victory brought into the house of the living God."

This message is thrilling! It is a message of certainty that the enemy will be overthrown; it is a message of confidence that many "testimonies of triumph" shall be garnered; and it is a message of security that those trophies of victory, those experiences of overcoming, shall not drop in shame to the ground for want of sufficient support to hold them up. We have a "Nail in a Sure Place."

LIVING THIS NAME

Common to our vernacular today are such expressions as "let down," "put-down," and "fallout." Each of these describes an undesirable result from the inability of one thing to sustain the weight of another.

"Someone let me down" expresses disappointment because a person proved undependable. "He really put me down" means one has been belittled. "Fallout" describes the negative aftermath of something, such as the release of radioactive material that the atmosphere is incapable of sustaining following a nuclear explosion. Looking at these contemporary terms in light of Isaiah's prophecy we discover several interesting truths.

First, resting today in Jesus, our Nail in a Sure Place, is our guarantee that we need not feel "let down" no matter what trials we experience. Second, because Christ alone is our security, we don't need to worry about being "put-down" by anyone. Finally, there's no need for negative "fallout" to pollute the growth we experience as long as we are secure in the confidence that Christ truly is our Nail in a Sure Place.

PRAYING THIS NAME

To pray in Jesus' name, our Nail in a Sure Place, is to recognize the full security Christ has gained for us through His matchless conquest of the power of sin, death, and hell. It is a security that is uniquely pictured in the actions of those ancient warrior-kings described in Isaiah's prophecy (Isa. 22).

These kings entered their temples to fasten a peg in a firm place. Jesus, through His death, resurrection, and ascension, has "entered the Most Holy Place once for all, having obtained eternal redemption . . . that those who are called may receive the promise of the eternal inheritance" (Heb. 9:12, 15). Christ has secured the promise of God's grace, forgiveness, and power toward us. He has entered the temple of God and fastened these provisions with a "steadfast nail." And that nail is His own life and blood, two realities that remain as changeless, unshakable, unmovable, infallible "testimonies of His triumph."

So, to pray today in Jesus' name, our Nail in a Sure Place, is to enter His courts and lay hold of Him as our "steadfast nail." It is to pray as Vicar John Newman prayed a century ago:

> O Lord, support us all the day long,
> until the shadows lengthen
> and the evening comes,

and the busy world is hushed,
and the fever of life is over,
and our work is done.
Then, Lord, in Your mercy
grant us a safe lodging,
and a holy rest, and peace at last;
through Jesus Christ
our Lord.[1]

TODAY'S PRAYER

As I approach Your holy throne today, Father,
I thank You that in the holy place of Your dwelling,
where I worship You now,
there are testimonies surrounding me
   that represent Your Son, Jesus,
and His great victory on my behalf.

In the name of Him whose finished triumph
   bears steadfast witness,
and whose victory—
   upon which I hang my hopes for tomorrow—
is won,
I rest secure,
knowing this Nail in a Sure Place will never let me down!

I praise You for this steadfast security
and for Your love that is providing it for me!
In Jesus' name.
Amen.

HALLOWING THIS NAME

Cover—Isa. 32:2
Fortress—Ps. 18:2
God of All Grace—1 Pet. 5:10
Hiding Place from the Wind—Isa. 32:2
Jehovah-Elohay (The Lord My God)—Zech. 14:5
Jehovah-Shammah (The Lord is There)—Ezek. 48:35
My Support—Ps. 18:18; 2 Sam. 22:19
My Stronghold—Nahum 1:7
Refuge from the Storm—Isa. 25:4

Sanctuary—Isa. 8:14
Shade from the Heat—Isa. 25:4
Sure Foundation—Isa. 28:16
Surety—Heb. 7:22
Your Shade—Ps. 121:5

5

A GREAT LIGHT
Isaiah 9:2

GUIDANCE

In *The Electronic Church* Archbishop Fulton J. Sheen wrote, "God does not show Himself equally to all creatures. This does not mean that He has favorites, that He decides to help some and to abandon others, but the difference occurs because it is impossible for Him to manifest Himself to certain hearts under the conditions they set up. Sunlight plays no favorites, but its reflection is very different on a lake than on a swamp."[1]

God, indeed, is ever searching for those who would draw back the curtain of their hearts to receive the full benefit of His guiding presence as "a Great Light." Quite simply, He is looking for listeners. As Francois Fenelon cautioned in *The Spiritual Letters*, "How can you expect God to speak in that gentle and inward voice which melts the soul, when you are making so much noise with your rapid reflections? Be silent and God will speak again."[2]

KNOWING THIS NAME

Few Old Testament prophets captured the vision of the coming Messiah as did Isaiah. By the revelation of the Holy Spirit, he foretold Christ as: being born of a virgin (7:14); God's anointed servant (42:1); the man of sorrows (53:3); the Redeemer (59:20);

one who is to be called Wonderful, Counselor, Everlasting Father, and Prince of Peace (9:6).

But somehow, amid this myriad display of traits and titles of the Messiah to come, His designation as a Great Light (9:2) seems to pass us as more a prophesied fact than a prophesied feature. It is, however, important to think carefully on this aspect of our Savior's personality. For in it we discover a vital truth for living a Christian life that daily depends on guidance from God.

Without pretense or vanity, Jesus told His contemporaries, "As long as I am in the world, I am the light of the world" (John 9:5). The setting in which He spoke these dramatic words is worthy of our recollection. Our Lord was just about to heal a man blind from birth. Somehow something of the entire episode reflects a condition afflicting us all. We are all born with a spiritual "birth defect"—we cannot see clearly the will and way of God for our lives. And it is only by an encounter with Jesus Christ that clear vision becomes ours. Scripture declares, "Unless one is born again, He cannot see the kingdom of God" (John 3:3). It is only in the light of Christ's person, presence, and power that we receive the knowledge of God (we perceive His fullness and reality, as well as our need of Him). The psalmist said, "In Your light we see light" (Ps. 36:9).

However, the prophecy Isaiah brought concerning a great light speaks even more specifically to our need than simply the promise of a revealing light sent to bring us the revelation of God. The blessedness of Isaiah's words have to do with a lesson learned from the geographical reference he makes. We read: "The land of Zebulun and the land of Naphtali . . . by the way of the sea, beyond the Jordan, in Galilee of the Gentiles" (Isa. 9:1).

The whole thrust of this prophetic promise (of a light shining to people in darkness) is that it refers to inhabitants of the land most distant from Jerusalem. Jebulun and Naphtali were tribal regions far to the north, whose boundaries were exceeded in distance from the capital city only by the tribe of Dan. Further reference is made to these tribes as living in an area called "the Galilee of the Gentiles," a term used because so many of the citizenry of the region were outside the covenant of God's people, Israel. And it is in these two statements that a beautiful truth emerges—a truth that helps us understand what it means to live (and pray) in Jesus' name, a Great Light.

LIVING THIS NAME

Scripture uses the image of light to assure us of many blessings vital to spiritual health. None, however, is of greater practical significance to daily Christian living than divine guidance. Frequently the Bible links light with guidance: "Your word is a lamp to my feet and a light to my path" (Ps. 119:105); "The entrance of Your words gives light" (Ps. 119:130); "Then God said, 'Let there be light'" (Gen. 1:3).

In the same sense that God "spoke" and light rushed forth to bring a new world with new growth, God still speaks "light" into the confusion and darkness of our daily circumstances. He is instantly at hand to show the way, to lead us in His light, to defuse the darkness around us.

But as sure as these promises are, there is something that seems even more personal and immediate to our human cry for a personal touch. In the words of Isaiah's prophecy, the light is not only spoken of, it is personified. The Messiah is that Light! His presence shines! Where He is, there is light—simply because He is there. To walk in Jesus is to walk in His light.

And what does all this mean in practical terms? For one thing, consider the reality of this light's penetration. Christ's glow reaches all the way to a "people who sat in darkness." The inference is that a lesser light would not have dispelled the shadows surrounding these people. Scripture declares, "Those who dwelt in the land of the shadow of death, upon them a light has shined" (Isa. 9:2). How readily can each of us identify with such a situation. All of us have faced those occasions when depression, weariness, or condemnation have engulfed us like a cloud. But suddenly Jesus—our Great Light—penetrates that cloud with His radiance, and we experience renewed vision as the glow of God's goodness sweeps away the oppressive cloud.

But beyond the light's power of penetration is its capacity for multiplication. Immediately after Isaiah describes the coming Messiah as a Great Light he says, "You have multiplied the nation and increased its joy; they rejoice before You according to the joy of harvest . . ." (Isa. 9:3). The message is obvious. When the cloud of oppression is dispelled, growth takes place in the same way that the sun causes a harvest to burst forth into fruition.

True, there is nothing so suffocating as the blanket of gloom that can encrust a human spirit in times of discouragement, disgrace, or disappointment. Sheer despair becomes compounded by the fruitlessness and the futility that often accompany that darkness. Soon it seems that everything about us withers, fades, and falls like a dead leaf or rotten fruit. Devoid of life-giving purpose, one begins to fall into despondency—and a smothering sense of hopelessness tempts us to believe we'll never be worth anything again.

But into this void the Spirit of God longs to breathe the overcoming testimony of Jesus, our Great Light. He wants to convince us that with this Light comes a brightness, a radiance, and a brilliance of divine ability to transform any circumstance and restore our purpose and fruitfulness. Our Great Light will multiply, increase joy, and bring a glorious harvest! It is God's promise fulfilled in Jesus, our Great Light, and it is our privilege not only to live in this Light, but to pray in its brilliance as well.

PRAYING THIS NAME

Praying in Jesus' name, a Great Light, means focusing the radiance of His person on the aspects of my day for which I desire divine guidance. Naturally, this involves a listening process in prayer. Writing in his *Journals*, Philosopher Søren Kierkegaard put this in perspective: "The unreflective person thinks and imagines that when he prays, the important thing, the thing he must concentrate upon, is that God should hear what he is praying for. And yet in the true, eternal sense, it is just the reverse; the true relation in prayer is not when God hears what is prayed for, but when the person continues to pray until he is the one who hears, who hears what God wills."[3] A more succinct way of saying this is that only those who linger really listen, for listening takes time.

So, praying in Jesus' name, a Great Light, is to linger long enough in Christ's presence to receive His revelation of God's best for us "today." And His best always begins with a revelation of what needs purifying in our lives. So let's begin our praying in Jesus' name today by agreeing with the humble African child who prayed:

> O Great Chief, light a candle within my heart that I may see what is therein, and sweep the rubbish from Your dwelling place.[4]

TODAY'S PRAYER

Guidance

This is my Savior, the Light of the World,
In whom is no shadow of turning.
No variability, ever the same,
Wondrous provision in His matchless Name,
I'm free from sin since He's taken my blame;
Now within me His love e'er is burning.

This Light of all lights shows the path I'm to take,
Be it thru brightest joy, dimmest sorrow.
The radiant peace that He gives doth insure,
Regardless of trials, foreboding, obscure.
In Him I've a resting place ever secure,
That gives gleaming hope for tomorrow.

The Light is the same on the Mount, in the vale,
And tho' life seems dark, still I know
His light has not faltered thru tests of the years,
It only seems flick'ring when I allow tears,
To overwhelm me in black moments of fear,
That bring gloom when trial's winds blow.

So look up to Him, for with eyes on the Light
One can't see the shadows surrounding.
Overcast skies will then soon become bright,
Tear-filled and misty eyes take on new sight,
For his hand on your heart will His love-flame ignite,
And You'll find life that's always abounding.

Jack W. Hayford.

HALLOWING THIS NAME

Chief Shepherd—1 Pet. 5:4
Friend Who Sticks Closer than a Brother—Prov. 18:24
Good Shepherd—John 10:11
Great Shepherd of the Sheep—Heb. 13:20
Jehovah-Rohi (The Lord My Shepherd)—Ps. 23:1
Light of Israel—Isa. 10:17
Light of Men—John 1:4
Light of the City—Rev. 21:23

Light to the Gentiles—Isa. 42:6; Luke 2:32
Light of the World—John 8:12
My Lamp—2 Sam. 22:29
My Shepherd—Ps. 23:1
One Shepherd—John 10:16
Shepherd—Gen. 49:24
Shepherd of Israel—Ps. 80:1
True Light—John 1:9
Your Everlasting Light—Isa. 60:20

6
A SCEPTER
Numbers 24:16-17

AUTHORITY

An old man living on a gentleman's estate in England was accustomed to using the wealthy baron's private walk when going to a nearby chapel. The man was in poor health and it saved him considerable time by taking this convenient route. Unfortunately, an unkind neighbor informed the baron of this repeated transgression and the baron began watching for the transgressor.

One day when the infirm man was walking to the house of God, he nearly bumped into the baron just as he entered his private path.

"What right have you to be on this path?" asked the baron.

"No right at all, sir," the elderly saint answered. "But I thought you wouldn't mind if an old man who has lived on your estate so many years used your private path to walk to God's house, especially as it's so much farther the other way."

"Give me your walking stick!" the baron said sternly. The trembling saint gave the man his stick, not knowing what to expect. To his surprise, the well-dressed gentlemen, with a kind smile, handed him his own walking stick, beautifully adorned with his family crest in solid gold.

"Here, my good man," said the baron in a gentle voice. "If anyone asks you again what right you have in walking this way, show them this crest and tell them I gave it to you!"

So it is with Jesus, who has given us the privilege and power to use His name. And further, according to Numbers 24:16-17, our Lord is described as "a Scepter" for all those who would choose to live and pray in His name.

KNOWING THIS NAME

A scepter is a staff, pole, or rodlike object held by a king as a symbol of His authority. Scepters come in varied lengths, and, although usually made of wood, they are often covered with precious metal and crowned with jewels. In Psalm 74:2 and Jeremiah 51:19 Israel is described as the Lord's *shaybet*, the Hebrew word for scepter. This same word is translated in the King James Version as "the rod of his inheritance." The next verse explains that God was going to use Israel as His instrument ("battle ax" or "war club") by which He would overthrow His enemies (see Jer. 51:19-23).

Although the King James Version translates *shaybet* in the above passages as "a rod," both the New King James Version and the New International Version translate the word in a more personal way as "the tribe of My inheritance."

So a scepter may involve more than merely an object—it also can refer to a person in whom authority is vested. This is even true in our time. For example, in modern day Britain the expression "to scepter" is used as a verb. When an offspring of a monarch is endowed with the same sovereign authority, it is said he or she is "sceptered," or invested with royal authority.

Interestingly, one of the clearest prophecies of the coming Messiah in all of Scripture (and our text for this lesson) is brought by one of its most ambivalent characters—Balaam. Several of the most quoted promises about the Messiah come from his lips. But like Judas, Balaam, who seems to have begun in the Spirit, falls into sin and dies as a tragic commentary on the effect of sinfulness. Nonetheless, it is Balaam who spoke these words by the Holy Spirit: "A Star shall come out of Jacob; a Scepter shall rise out of Israel, and batter the brow of Moab, and destroy all the sons of tumult" (Num. 24:17).

The significance of this prophecy at the time it was given was that Moab was the most immediate obstacle for hindering Israel's wilderness progress. En route toward their promised possession, Israel was being hindered by the troops of Moab. In this prophecy, God was saying that this present adversary ultimately would be cast down by reason of a promised Ruler—a Scepter—who would some day rise out of Israel.

Every Bible scholar acknowledges that this prophecy foretells the coming Messiah. Christ is that Scepter of authority. And He Himself declared, "All authority has been given to Me in heaven and on earth" (Matt. 28:18). Paul adds, "He is the head . . . that in all things He may have the preeminence" (Col. 1:18). Thus, having been "exalted to the right hand of God" (Acts 2:33), Christ Himself has become the representation—the Incarnate Scepter— of the living God's total authority over all things in this world and in the world to come, including earth, heaven, and even hell itself. As Kathe Wood's simple chorus "Lord of Heaven, Lord of Earth" proclaims:

> He is Lord of heaven,
> Lord of earth;
> Lord of all that ever shall be;
> Lord of heaven,
> Lord of earth;
> Lord of all that is to come.

LIVING THIS NAME

Our best understanding of the practical meaning of Christ, our Scepter of authority, is perhaps best summed up in the moving account of Esther, a young woman who faced the crisis of a potential holocaust some four hundred years before Christ. Just as this young Jewess was being crowned the bride of Persia's emperor, Ahasuerus, the entire Jewish race was scheduled for annihilation throughout the Persian empire. Naturally, Esther wanted to plead for justice and deliverance for her people, but she faced a serious dilemma. Access to the king's court was by invitation only—even for the queen. To enter his throne room uninvited was to risk immediate death. And yet the crisis would not wait for an invitation.

The story of the entire book bearing the queen's name turns on that telling moment when Esther ventures into the court on her own initiative. For a few anxious moments the fate of an entire nation hangs in the balance. Suddenly Ahasuerus acts. Lovingly he extends his scepter and invites Esther to approach him and touch it.

The action of extending the scepter meant that Esther had been received into the king's favor, and that her request need only be spoken. The queen had touched the symbol of authority and every power represented in that scepter was now at her disposal.

PRAYING THIS NAME

And so it is when we come to the Father in Jesus' name, our promised Scepter, our access to God's holiest of holies is insured by open invitation. "Let us therefore come boldly to the throne of grace . . ." (Heb. 4:16). We have a Savior who is able to "sympathize with our weaknesses" (Heb. 4:15) and by whose almightiness our most demanding obstacle may be faced in the authority of His name, our Scepter.

To pray with this kind of authority is to pray as Martin Luther prayed in 1540 when his close friend Frederick Myconius lay dying. Attending physicians had given Myconius only a few days to live, and so he wrote a farewell letter to Luther, his cherished friend.

When Luther received the letter he was so incensed that Frederick Myconius would consider "dying on him" at such a crucial time in the reformation of the Church that he immediately sat down and wrote a fearless reply. Assured within that God would keep his friend alive at least long enough to receive his response, Martin Luther wrote these astounding words: "I command thee in the name of God to live because I still have need of thee in the work of reforming the church! The Lord will never let me hear that thou art dead, but will permit thee to survive me." The brief but poignant letter concluded, "For this I am praying, this is my will and may my will be done—because I seek only to glorify the name of God."

Not only did Myconius live long enough to receive Luther's reply, but the moment he read the reformer's authoritative words he felt as if God Himself had breathed new life into his body. In a few days Myconius was restored to complete health and ultimately outlived Luther by two months!

Thus, praying today in Jesus' name, our Scepter, is praying with the full authority God invested in His Son. Just as Christ commanded situations to change by His authority, so we can command obstacles to move by that same authority simply because this privilege has been extended to us.

When Jesus told His disciples to "ask anything in my name" (John 14:13-14) He used a Greek expression that also can mean "make a claim based on my name." To understand precisely what Jesus meant in using these words consider the record of the early church and the way Jesus' disciples interpreted the words, for they heard Jesus speak them in their own language.

The first recorded instance of Christ's disciples "claiming" or "using" His name is found in Acts 3 where we discover Peter and John visiting the temple for prayer. As they approached the gate a crippled man pleads for financial aid. Boldly Peter assumes what might be described as an authoritative "prayer stance" (see Acts 3:6). And although some might question whether this is prayer at all, it clearly is an instance of exercising "the power of attorney" given by Christ to His disciples in the Upper Room just hours before He went to Gethsemane.

Note carefully the nature of Peter's prayer. He doesn't expressly ask God to do anything in Jesus' name; rather he makes a claim based on Christ's name. He employs the authority of Jesus' name and commands the crippled man to rise and walk. Seconds later, but only after Peter actually lifts him up, a further act of authority, the man goes "walking, and leaping, and praising God" (Acts 3:8).

So exercising our authority in Jesus' name, our Scepter, may go beyond merely asking our Lord to grant a particular request. It may mean we actually command a situation to change in Jesus' name simply because Christ has already given us that authority. He said, "Whoever says to this mountain, 'Be removed' . . . and does not doubt in his heart . . . he shall have whatever he says" (Mark 11:23).

TODAY'S PRAYER

I come to You, Father,
to praise You and to express my humility
over the fact that You have arranged for my exaltation.
It is too much for me to bear at times;
as I think how readily You share the power
of Your throne with Your redeemed.

This day I open my life to Your Holy Spirit
to help me live in the dimensions of Jesus' name—
the Scepter.

I reach to touch Your power and Your authority,
that my need and my fears may be overcome
in those mighty resources.
Lord Jesus, I reach to touch You with the gratitude
of knowing You are touchable—
that You know my feelings, and You are sensitive
to every need, pain, or cry.

And, Holy Spirit, I welcome Your assistance.
Help me to so live this day in the name of
him who is the Scepter,
that I may rise above all power and dominion
that would seek
to drag me down or defeat me.

Through Jesus' triumph and power I take the
place of authority He has given me—
as I live in Him—
in Jesus' name!
Amen.

HALLOWING THIS NAME

Blessed and Only Potentate—1 Tim. 6:15
Crown of Glory—Isa. 28:5
Diadem of Beauty—Isa. 28:5
Ensign of the People—Isa. 11:10 (KJV)
Faithful Witness—Rev. 1:5
Glorious Throne to His Father's House—Isa. 22:23
Jehovah-Nissi (The Lord My Banner)—Exod. 17:15
King of Glory—Ps. 24:10
King of Kings—Rev. 17:14
King of the Saints—Rev. 15:3
King over All the Earth—Zech. 14:9
One Who Shall Have Dominion—Num. 24:19
Polished Shaft—Isa. 49:2
Prince of Princes—Dan. 8:25
Rod of Your Strength—Ps. 110:2
Rod from the Stem of Jesse—Isa. 11:1
Ruler—Micah 5:2

7

A QUICKENING SPIRIT
1 Corinthians 15:45

VITALITY

Years ago a minister made an unfortunate mistake as he conducted a funeral. Before him in an open casket lay the remains of the departed brother. Motioning toward the deceased and speaking in somber tones the preacher said, "This corpse has been a member of my church for ten years."

Sadly, the Church appears to be filled with spiritual corpses—those who lack divine vitality. They may attend church, even occasionally read their Bibles and pray, but they lack a real quality of spiritual life. They're not too unlike those Christians pictured by a young girl who was trying to describe her preacher's sermon to her parents, who had been unable to attend church that morning. "I really can't remember much that he preached," said the child, "but I think his text was, 'Many were cold and a few were frozen.'"

But praise God, beloved, a thaw is coming for those who would learn to pray in the energy and vitality of Jesus' name, a "Quickening Spirit" (1 Cor. 15:45). All of the divine energy that flows from God's essence is available in Jesus' name, and God never "slumbers or sleeps" (Ps. 121:4). As Henry Ward Beecher observed, "The most intensely thoughtful and most intensely active being in the universe is God. He is never weary of His work."[1]

47

KNOWING THIS NAME

There is a haunting phrase from the prophecies of Isaiah which captivates one's imagination: "Stop trusting in man, who has but a breath in his nostrils" (Isa. 2:22, NIV). The related passage is an announcement by God to His messenger, Isaiah, that the strength, pride, and pomp of man's finest and best is ultimately destined for failure. This conclusion is announced in those words "Stop trusting in man . . . breath . . . nostrils." The poetic phraseology obviously suggests this paraphrase: "Don't depend upon the resources of anyone whose sole source of energy is the common breath of the average man. If his only life-breath is that which passes through his nose, he is without the life-breath that proceeds from the Spirit of God."

In contrast to man's limited dimension of breathing (just air), the writer of 1 Corinthians points to another dimension of energy—the breath of the Holy Spirit which proceeds to us through the person of Jesus. Paul writes: "The first man Adam became a living being. The last Adam became a life-giving (quickening, KJV) spirit. However, the spiritual is not first, but the natural, and afterward the spiritual. The first man was of the earth, made of dust; the second Man is the Lord from heaven" (1 Cor. 15:45-47).

Held in stark contrast are two races and two sources of sustained strength. First is Adam's fallen race, a race at the created level sustained by the breathing of air. Second is Christ's reborn race, a people at the redeemed level sustained by the breath of the Holy Spirit.

All of us experience the first resource. Since creation when "God breathed into man's nostrils the breath of life and man became a living soul" (Gen. 2:7), we all have depended upon our respiratory systems for survival. If breathing is denied for more than a few minutes, it usually results in at least some deterioration of certain brain functions. If air is denied too long, death is imminent. We are all creatures "whose breath is in our nostrils." But there is an added dimension of living energy (life-sustaining "breath") available to all whom Jesus has redeemed.

Consider the account following Christ's resurrection when He came into the room where His disciples were hiding in fear. It is interesting to note one of His first actions. Now that the process of salvation, through Christ's death and resurrection, was completed, Jesus operated as Lord of their new order. The Bible says, "He

breathed on them, and said to them, 'Receive the Holy Spirit' "
(John 20:22). This is clearly a direct parallel of the first creation,
when the Father had created man and then endued him with life-
breath. Now a new creation has been made possible. The Son of
God from heaven has become man's Redeemer and now is making possible man's recovery from the limits imposed upon him by
reason of sin and man's devastating fall from his originally intended order. All that "the first Adam" could bequeath to his
offspring has now been exceeded by everlasting life available
only through "the Second Adam"—the Lord Jesus Christ. By
reason of His resurrection, He now transmits a life-breath that
gives spiritual vitality far beyond the limits of unredeemed man.

LIVING THIS NAME

Most of us have been pressed into action by haste-filled situations
where we've had to run until breath was no longer available.
Winded, we stop, bending over to nurse the pain in our sides.
Gasping for breath, chests heaving and lungs burning, we've
reached our limit. David describes this sensation in his words, "As
the deer pants for the water brooks, so pants my soul for You, O
God" (Ps. 42:1). And that is exactly where we should go—to the
Lord!

Our Savior is a quickening spirit—a revitalizing, breath-of-life-
giving "resuscitator" of weary souls. When your spiritual breath
rate seems too heavy and the pace impossible, it's probably a sign
that you're functioning only with Adam's race, a race whose
breath is in its nostrils. What we all need is "spirit-breath," and in
Jesus' name, our Quickening Spirit, it is available.

PRAYING THIS NAME

To pray in Jesus' name, our Quickening Spirit, is to stop periodically and take a deep breath of His fresh, supernatural, "life-
giving" air. It is to "catch our breath" in His promise: "Those who
wait on the Lord shall renew their strength; they shall mount up
with wings like eagles, they shall run and not be weary, they shall
walk and not faint" (Isa. 40:31). Here a promise of spiritual
vitality is linked to waiting upon the Lord. We're called to slow
down in the Lord. St. Francis of Sales in his *Letters to Persons in
Religion* suggested centuries ago, "Just walk on uninterruptedly

and very quietly; if God makes you run, He will enlarge your heart."[2]

To pray in Jesus' name, our Quickening Spirit, is to implement, through prayer, the thought of Proverbs 18:21: "Death and life are in the power of the tongue." In Jesus' name we can speak death to whatever is robbing us of energy and vitality (whether it be spiritual, physical, or material) while at the same time speaking life into situations or circumstances that need those same qualities. For example, we can speak death in Jesus' name to resentment that may be destroying a marriage and life into the loving affection that once existed, even though it may seem to have long since disappeared.

Beyond that, praying in Jesus' name, our Quickening Spirit, means using the power of His name to awaken our own spirits in daily renewal. It is to pray with the psalmist, "Revive me, O Lord, for Your name's sake" (Ps. 143:11). To that we might add Dwight L. Moody's prayer:

> Use me then, my Savior, for whatever purpose, and in whatever way, You may require. Here is my poor heart, an empty vessel; fill it with Your grace. Here is my sinful and troubled soul; quicken it and refresh it with Your love. Take my heart for Your abode; my mouth to spread abroad the glory of Your Name; my love and all my powers, for the advancement of Your believing people; and never suffer the steadfastness and confidence of my faith to abate; so that at all times I may be enabled from the heart to say, "Jesus needs me, and I am His."[3]

TODAY'S PRAYER

Lord,
I come today as a part of Your New Creation.
I praise You for the newness into which You've ushered me—
new joy, because You've forgiven me;
new hope, because of Your promises to me; and
new love, because You first loved me.

But Lord, I am also very conscious of the finite limits of my flesh.
Though part of a New Creation,
I am also a creature of Adam's race.
Oftentime my spirit is willing but my flesh is weak.

And so I come to this day to receive Your inbreathing—
the inflow of the life-breath of Your Spirit.
You know how it was that You breathed into Adam long ago,
and the First Creation sprang to life.
Now, O Lord—O life-giving, Quickening Spirit—
breathe freshness and newness of life into me.
Let Your Spirit refresh me at my points of weariness,
and by Your Spirit strengthen me beyond my weakness.
In Jesus' name.
Amen.

HALLOWING THIS NAME

Christ Our Life—Col. 3:4
Firstfruits of Those Who Have Fallen Asleep—1 Cor. 15:20
Fountain of Living Waters—Jer. 17:13-14
God of My Life—Ps. 42:8
He Who Lives—Rev. 1:18
Horn of Salvation—Luke 1:69
Judge of the Living and the Dead—Acts 10:42
Lord of Both the Dead and the Living—Rom. 14:9
My Strength—2 Sam. 22:33
Prince of Life—Acts 3:15
Resting Place—Jer. 50:6
Restorer—Ps. 23:3
Resurrection—John 11:25
Strength of My Life—Ps. 27:1
Way, the Truth, and the Life—John 14:6

8
THE HEAD OF THE BODY
Colossians 1:18

SUPERVISION

An eminent architect was under cross-examination at a trial concerning a building he had designed. One of the prosecutors, attempting to distract the man during his testimony, asked, "Are you a builder?"

Immediately the witness replied, "No, sir, I am an architect."

"But they are much the same, aren't they?" the prosecutor added.

"I beg your pardon, sir, but in my opinion they are totally different."

"Oh, indeed! Perhaps you will explain the difference?"

To this the witness responded, "An architect, sir, conceives the design, prepares the plan, draws all to specifications, and in short, supplies the mind. The builder is merely the bricklayer or the carpenter. The builder is the machine; the architect, the power that puts it together and sets it going."

"Oh, very well, Mr. Architect, that will do. And now, after your very ingenious distinction between the two, perhaps you can inform the court who was the architect of the Tower of Babel?"

The witness promptly responded, "There was no architect, sir, only builders. That's why there was so much confusion."

God knew the church needed a head. For this reason Christ was given as the Head of the body. He is our supervisor. And being the head, He also is our mind or, to use a colloquial expression, "the brains of the operation."

Christ, in fact, supervised creation itself. Scripture states, "For by Him all things were created that are in heaven and that are on earth" (Col. 1:16). In his essay "On the Existence of God," Francois Fenelon wrote, "Let us study the visible creation as we will; take the anatomy of the smallest animal; look at the smallest grain of corn that is planted in the earth, and the manner in which its germ produces and multiplies; observe attentively the rosebud, how carefully it opens to the sun, and closes at its setting; and we shall see more skill and design than in all the works of man."[1]

KNOWING THIS NAME

If you ever travel to England, be prepared to meet Paddington Bear. Somewhat like Winnie the Pooh, Paddington Bear is an interesting and humorous character. His name is derived from Paddington Station, one of London's primary train terminals where this fictional bear is said to have arrived from Peru, tagged only with the words, "Please look after this bear." And everywhere these little teddy-bear-like Paddingtons are sold they carry the same inscription—an appeal, to whomever the little stuffed toy comes, to "look after him."

There is something homey and touching about these words. All of us recognize the need for someone to "look after" us. It isn't simply a matter of a childhood need, for even honest adults are aware that one never outgrows the need for supervision. So it can be a very gratifying thing to discover that watchful and authoritative supervision is a distinct function of Christ's ministry. As Scripture states, "He is the head of the body, the church" (Col. 1:18).

Of course, we more commonly understand that this title of our Lord refers to His right to administrate and direct the affairs of His whole church. Whether we are dealing with the church globally or in a local congregation, Christ is its Architect, Builder, and Lord. But examined more closely, the words, "head of the body, the church" (Col. 1:18) also clearly include Christ's personal headship over each member of His body. In the same way that the Bible describes the husband as "the head of the wife" (Eph. 5:23), pointing out that he is lovingly responsible for her best interests, so Jesus, our Head, is fully committed to each of us who constitute His bride—the church.

Unfortunately there is a tendency by some to think of headship as being authoritarian or heavy-handed. It's as though they believe being "the head" gives them the right to be indifferently bossy or cruelly insensitive to those under their supervision. Because of this misconception, some of us who know Jesus as our Savior actually fear to acknowledge Him as our Head.

This misunderstanding manifests itself in the ways some of us face various details of life. Too often we fear bringing certain details before Him in humble acknowledgment of His right to supervise and direct our behavior. Because we have been exploited at one time or another by someone who was in a supervisory capacity over us (even an unkind parent), we somehow feel that Christ may abuse His awesome authority over us.

If you find yourself in this position, it might help you to find victory over such fear if you draw an analogy from your own physical body's relationship to your physical "head."

Your head—the core of your powers of reason and reflex—is a prime example of the care and concern for the body which any sane, sober head employs. The fact that your head has the power of control over your body does not make your head indifferent or insensitive to your body's needs, feelings, or fulfillment. To the contrary, your head: (1) thinks of ways to better your body's circumstances (brings improvement); (2) perceives those things that might injure your body and avoids them (provides protection); and (3) designs ways and programs that will serve your body's needs (gives assistance). Consider those activities of your head—improvement, protection, and assistance—and then ask yourself, "Is Jesus less thoughtful about His body than I am of mine?"

LIVING THIS NAME

Because our Lord is ever-present, we must recognize that He, the Head of the Body, is always with us no matter where we go. And even though this ever-present "Supervisor" most often stands beside us in silence, He is nonetheless present, available on a moment's notice to those who would simply acknowledge His nearness. Sadly, too few of us have developed the habit cultivated by Brother Lawrence, the sixteenth-century monk, who learned to "practice the presence of God." We fail to realize our spiritual "head" is with us wherever we go just as our physical head is attached to our physical body.

As philosopher Søren Kierkegaard wrote in his *Journals:* "The remarkable thing about the way in which people talk about God, or about their relations to God, is that it seems to escape them completely that God hears what they are saying."[2]

To live in the recognition that Jesus is the Head of the Body is to live with a continuing realization that we are an organic part of that body. To function in "health" we must receive supervision from our Head. This involves far more than a mere casual communion with Christ. Consider the very components of the word *supervision*. *Vision* refers to the capacity and ability to perceive or see; *super* means "from above." Because Jesus is with us today, no matter where we may go we have the capacity to "see from above." We can see things as Jesus sees them if we look through His eyes. Thus, to rely on Jesus, the Head of the Body, is to rely on His supervision in all we do.

PRAYING THIS NAME

Teresa of Avila, the sixteenth-century "praying nun" founded a spiritual order of nuns called "the barefoot Carmelites." She sought only those candidates who possessed a passionate hunger for more of God coupled with a willingness to work with all their might.

One of Teresa's shortest recorded prayers reveals both her some-times blunt nature and her recognition of the frailties of the human species: "God preserve us from stupid nuns!" Equally brief was her practical prayer, "From silly devotions and from sour-faced saints, good Lord deliver us."[3]

Yet it was this giant of the faith who, at a dark time in an indulgent church, realized Christ had no other means but His church to change our world. And so she cautioned her Order:

> Christ has no body now on earth but yours; yours are the only hands with which He can do His work, yours are the only feet with which He can go about the world, yours are the only eyes through which His compassion can shine forth upon a troubled world.
>
> Christ has no body now on earth but yours.[4]

So, to pray today in Jesus' name as our Head is to acknowledge Him during prayer as the supervisor of each task we undertake. Christ alone is the Architect and Builder of our days. In Him there will be no towering Babels of confusion, for "God is not the author of confusion but of peace" (1 Cor. 14:33).

TODAY'S PRAYER

Savior,
I'm so glad that I'm joined to You.
What confidence I am privileged to enjoy, Lord Jesus,
since You have made me one with Yourself.
And, according to the Father's word,
I am complete in You!

I enter this day, with its challenges,
its problems,
its unknowns.
I enter it linked to You.
I acknowledge You as my Head—
able to direct me,
ready to protect me,
certain to help me, and
faithful to nurture me.
With praise to You, the doorway to today opens before me,
and I have no hesitation about walking forward.
Each step is directed by You—my living Head—
my Lord and Savior, Jesus Christ,
In Your name.
Amen.

HALLOWING THIS NAME

Author and Finisher of Faith—Heb. 12:2
Commander—Isa. 55:4
Commander of the Army of the Lord—Josh. 5:14
Head of Every Man—1 Cor. 11:3
Head over All Things—Eph. 1:22
Judge of the Living and the Dead—Acts 10:42
Leader—Isa. 55:4
Master of the House—Luke 13:25
My Helper—Heb. 13:6
My Shepherd—Ps. 23:1
Our Lawgiver—Isa. 33:22

Our Potter—Isa. 64:8
Ruler—Matt. 23:8
Shepherd and Overseer of Your Souls—1 Pet 2:25
Spirit of Judgment—Isa. 28:5-6
Teacher—Matt. 23:8; John 13:13
Your Keeper—Ps. 121:5

9
THE LORD OF PEACE
2 Thessalonians 3:16

COMFORT

St. Ignatius Loyola in compiling his *Spiritual Exercises* wrote, "In times of dryness and desolation we must be patient, and wait with resignation for the return of consolation, putting our trust in the goodness of God. We must animate ourselves by the thought that God is always with us, that He only allows this trial for our greater good, and that we have not necessarily lost His grace because we have lost the taste and feeling of it."[1]

Comfort or consolation is the outflowing of the peace quality of God's divine nature. Our Lord not only possesses peace, His very nature is peace. And, as Loyola suggests, we may have lost the taste and feeling of God's grace, but that changes nothing of the nature and character of our Lord. He is still infinitely the same, and His grace abounds whether we feel it or not.

True, there are those times when Satan's arguments tend to paint a picture of the Lord as being absent. But like all of Satan's arguments, these are merely additional lies from the "father of lies" (John 8:44). God may, indeed, be silent, but He is never absent. He feels every hurt and senses every pain. As Søren Kierkegaard wisely assessed, "He who loves God has no need that others weep for him. He forgets his suffering in love, forgets it so thoroughly that no one even suspects his pain except Thee, O God, who seest in secret, and knowest each need, and countest the tears and forgettest nothing."[2]

Said simply, he who knows the Lord knows peace, for Jesus Christ is the Lord of Peace (2 Thess. 3:16).

KNOWING THIS NAME

When Paul concluded his second letter to the Christians at Thessalonica he added this benediction, "Now may the Lord of peace Himself give you peace always in every way. The Lord be with you all" (2 Thess. 3:16). It is here that we find yet another name for our glorious Savior: The Lord of Peace.

There are three things about these benedictory words of Paul that make them delightfully special: their intimacy, constancy, and supremacy.

First, *notice the intimacy of Paul's picture of peace.* The Lord Himself promises to give it. No second-hand delivery method is to be employed. This is one case where Jesus does not choose an angelic messenger to bring His promise. He will do it Himself—a picture of personal intimacy.

Second, *note the constancy of Paul's promise of peace.* We read, "The Lord . . . give you peace always." There are often unpredictable turns in the road of life that each of us pursue. And at various points along the path we may encounter such obstacles as turmoil, strife, and discord. But Paul promises that at every point in our progress peace will prevail. That's a picture of true constancy.

Finally, *consider the supremacy of Paul's promise of peace.* The Apostle says, "The Lord . . . give you peace always in every way." This is no ordinary peace, it is "peace supreme." Note how our Creator commits Himself to fashion His own unique "measure of peace" for every troubling situation we may encounter. Whatever facet of the diamond of God's peace that we need to brighten our days or comfort our hearts, Christ is the Master (Lord) of peace and is fully capable of infusing His peace into those circumstances.

It is interesting to note the various times in Scripture when certain provisions are promised by our Lord and then underwritten by a statement that He is either the Lord, God, or Father of that particular quality or trait. For example, in 2 Corinthians 1:3 we read, "Blessed be the God and Father of our Lord Jesus Christ, the Father of mercies and God of all comfort."

Note "the Father of mercies and God of all comfort." In other words, mercy and comfort are not merely promised, they are insured as being available in and through the one who offers them and controls the entire resource of them. This is the Bible's way of saying, "There will never be a shortage of either mercy or comfort; there will never be a restriction. God has the monopoly on them both!"

In 2 Thessalonians 3:16 the same thing is said of peace. Christ is the Lord of Peace and He is master and controller of that peace. Thus He can provide an unlimited supply of it.

LIVING THIS NAME

The basic idea implied in the Greek word for peace, *eireney*, is unity or wholeness. We sometimes use the word *composure* to express a person's feeling of being "all together." When that sense of inner unity is broken, we describe it as being "unpeaceful." It is into such situations that Christ, our Lord of Peace, breathes wholeness, something He does in three specific ways.

First, *Jesus breathes calm into troubled situations.* Consider the unforgettable words Christ spoke to a raging storm: "Peace, be still!" (Mark 4:39). His authority over creation was magnificently displayed, to the awe and wonder of a handful of frightened disciples.

"What manner of man is this," they said, "that even the wind and the sea obey Him?" (Mark 4:41, KJV). The following verses say that "a great calm" followed, a calm that was a second miracle in its own right. It was miraculous enough that the wind stopped, but after any storm, waves usually continue to lash the shoreline for hours. Not so when the Lord of Peace speaks a word of peace. There is immediate calm in Jesus' name. As Madame Guyon said poetically:

> To me remains no place nor time;
> My country is in every clime;
> I can be calm and free from care
> On any shore, since God is there.[3]

Second, *Jesus breathes unity into troubled situations.* "We have peace with God through our Lord Jesus Christ," Paul tells us (Rom. 5:1). When the quiet of your soul is assaulted, the ultimate point of refuge is your relationship with the Father. As basic and foundational as it is, there is no greater truth in the gospel than this: In Jesus' name we have been joined together with the heart of God.

And He whose heart reached down to us in Christ actually has been knit together with us through Christ! We not only have a Savior who calms the storms of life, but in Christ we "have an anchor" that securely positions us permanently in a safe harbor (Heb. 6:19).

Finally, *Jesus breathes reconciliation into troubled situations.* Paul wrote, "He Himself is our peace, who has made both one . . ." (Eph. 2:14). The beauty of our salvation is that every attribute of it not only is revealed to us, but the Holy Spirit has a means of working those same qualities in and through us. And so the unity with the Father into which Christ has brought us is designed to work a unifying grace between us and others. The Lord of Peace is able to reconcile us to anyone with whom we may have experienced difficulty or hostility. Ephesians 2:14-17 speaks of the breaking down of sectarianism, racism, and religious dissension. Today we are not only called to love one another in Jesus' name, but we are given a resource for reconciliation through prayer.

Take comfort, loved one. There is no stress, no test, no person who can successfully resist prayer that invites the Lord of Peace to work His calm, unity, and reconciliation. Christ is the Lord of every situation, and He will rule in that circumstance until it is brought completely under His mastery.

PRAYING THIS NAME

When we pray in Jesus' name, the Lord of Peace, we speak the provision of His peace and comfort into each potentially disturbing situation in the day. This is not to say we will always be successful in commanding a situation to change; God may even have a specific purpose for the tears or difficulties. As Henry Ward Beecher preached, "God washes the eyes by tears until they can behold the invisible land where tears shall come no more."[4] Frederick Faber in *Spiritual Conferences* adds, "Difficulties are the stones out of which all God's houses are built."[5] What we *can* do is speak God's peace into the conflict.

It could be that God sometimes allows difficulties and sorrows so we might "long" after more of Jesus, our Lord of Peace. So when, as the result of prayer, a sense of peace finally floods our being, we must not overlook the fact that we aren't feeling peace so much as the presence of Christ, who is our peace. In his *Treatise*, Francis of Sales advised, "There is a great difference between being occupied with God who gives us the contentment, and of being busied with the contentment which God gives us."[6]

So today as you pray in Jesus' name, the Lord of Peace, you are moving into God's divine rest through your petitions. You can pray expectantly in the spirit of Christina Rossetti's nineteenth-century prayer:

O Lord, Jesus Christ,
who art as the shadow of a great rock in a weary land,
who beholdest Thy weak creatures
weary of labor, weary of pleasure,
weary of hope deferred, weary of self;
in thine abundant compassion,
and fellow feeling with us,
and unutterable tenderness,
bring us, we pray Thee, unto Thy rest.[7]

TODAY'S PRAYER

Help, Lord!
My world today seems like Galilee at tempest time.
I feel very small and in the middle—
with something of the feeling that my boat is paper-thin
and the waves are steel scissors.
I know You care, Jesus, but today I must confess
I think I understand the disciples outcry:
"Master—don't You care that we're sinking?"

Forgive my fears,
for I know they are sad commentaries on my faith—
that is, my faithlessness.
I come to You, announcing my true belief:
You, Lord Jesus Christ, are the Lord of Peace.
I turn to You and from the storm.
I look to You and away from fear.
Today I step into the resources of Your name—
Prince of Peace—whose rule is able to overthrow
the factors that fret my soul and force my fears.

Stand tall within me, Jesus.
Rise up and denounce the winds—Be still!

And in Your almighty name I welcome
calmness,
wholeness, and
harmony.
Praise Your name, Lord Jesus.
Amen.

HALLOWING THIS NAME

Consolation of Israel—Luke 2:25
God of All Comfort—2 Cor. 1:3
God of Love and Peace—2 Cor. 13:11
God of Patience and Comfort—Rom. 15:5
God of Peace—Rom. 15:33
Great Shepherd of the Sheep—Heb. 13:20
Hope of Israel—Jer. 17:13
Jehovah-Shalom (The Lord Our Peace)—Judg. 6:24
King of Peace—Heb. 7:2
Man of Sorrows—Isa. 53:3
My Hope—Ps. 71:5
My Shepherd—Ps. 23:1
Our Peace—Eph. 2:14
Peace Offering—Lev. 3:1-5
Prince of Peace—Isa. 9:6
Resting Place—Jer. 50:6
Shepherd—Gen. 49:24
Shiloh (Peacemaker)—Gen. 49:10
Strength to the Needy—Isa. 25:4

10
THE BRIGHTNESS
OF HIS GLORY
Hebrews 1:3

EXCELLENCE

In suggesting we imitate Christ, Thomas à Kempis offered this prayer, "O everlasting Light, surpassing all created luminaries, flash forth Thy lightning from above, piercing all the most inward parts of my heart. Make clean, make glad, make bright, and make alive my spirit, with all the powers thereof, that I may cleave unto Thee in ecstasies of joy."[1]

Jesus, alone, is the brightness of the glory of the Lord. He is the reflection of God's immeasurable excellence. And everywhere we look we see this glory. As Henry Ward Beecher wrote, "Nature would be scarcely worth a puff of the empty wind if it were not that all nature is but a temple, of which God is the brightness and the glory."[2]

KNOWING THIS NAME

Glory refers to that which exceeds or excels. The glory of a craftsman is his ability to use the ordinary to create the extraordinary. The glory of an athlete is his ability to use his skill to seize the moment and turn it into the magnificent: a home run, a touchdown, a goal, a great catch, or a run across the finish line ahead of the pack.

Residing in every human heart are dreams of glory, although

the realities of life and the limitations of our flesh tend to quench our desire to attain these dreams. But Christ has come to bring every one of us into His glory. He wants to give us the capacity to obtain what has seemed unapproachable and unattainable (Heb. 2:10). In Jesus' name, the Brightness of God's Glory, we can experience and know *real* glory!

There is a recurring call in our society to a spirit of excellence. This call is amplified by the current tendency of being satisfied with mediocrity. All of us are tempted to settle for less than the finest (merely "good" has become the enemy of "best"). And our own sense of limitation often argues for that settlement. But Christ has called us to glory. He appeals to us to allow His excellence to shine through us until everything that is unworthy of His presence is crowded out.

Most of us feel the daily pressures that give way to the commonplace, the shabby, or the second-rate. Yet, the Bible tells us that Christ "in us" affords "the hope of glory" (Col. 1:27). This promise not only focuses on an eternal future in the glory of His presence, but on a present measure of the glory of Christ working His splendor in and through us.

The writer to the Hebrews states that Christ Himself is the fullest manifestation and representation of God's glory (Heb. 1:3). Or, as Paul suggests, we have seen "the glory of God in the face of Jesus Christ" (2 Cor. 4:6). In the person of Jesus we have been presented with the ultimate of God's excellence. Christ is the best, He cannot be excelled. He is a complete picture of excellence, of all that man can hope to become. And it is in the light of this excellence that we can confront in ourselves whatever limits us from rising to the fullest and the finest we can be in Him.

LIVING THIS NAME

The human approach to a daily quest for excellence is often wearying. It is plagued with perfectionism, criticism, and competition. The divine way, however, is restful, filled with grace, goodness, and mercy. It ensures a way to experience and live in the excellence of God's glory without the snags and snares of a human approach. But to experience this glory we must heed a threefold call.

First, *we are called to expect Christ's excellence.* In 2 Corinthians 3 we discover a detailed development of the superiority of the New Testament resource over the Old Testament provision. Paul notes that the Old Testament demonstration and release of God's power was so mighty that Moses' face was set aglow by it. Then he goes on to describe the New Testament demonstration and release of the Holy Spirit as "the glory that excels" (2 Cor. 3:10). The climax of the passage is a statement concerning our beholding and being changed by the brightness of Christ's excellence—"from glory to glory" (2 Cor. 3:18). It is a promise that invites our expectation.

Second, *we are called to approach Christ's excellence.* The overwhelming brightness of God's throne is described vividly in John's revelation (see Rev. 4:5). Earlier, in Revelation 1, the radiance of Christ's person is described. Studying those scenes and seeing John's response as he falls before such majesty helps us capture a sense of what is meant by Paul's description of Christ in 1 Timothy 6:15-16:

> He who is the blessed and only Potentate, the King of kings and Lord of lords, who alone has immortality, dwelling in unapproachable light, whom no man has seen or can see, to whom be honor and everlasting power. Amen.

The unapproachableness of such excellence and glory would intimidate us in our quest except for one fact: God's grace has opened the door for our approach! Unredeemed man at His best can never become worthy of approach. But the brightness of God's glorious excellence displayed to us in Jesus Christ has not only manifested that glory but has made a way for us to enter into it! The Psalmist said, "Blessed is the man whom You choose, and cause to approach You, that he may dwell in Your courts. We shall be satisfied with the goodness of Your house, of Your holy temple" (Ps. 65:4).

Finally, *we are called to witness and experience Christ's excellence.* No episode in the Bible is more stirring than Isaiah's description of the glory of God in the temple (Isa. 6:1-8). Here the prophet outlines a complete message on the awesomeness, the awareness, and the action of God's excellence. In Isaiah's experience we discover a road map of sorts just waiting to lead us to the glory of the Lord. If we follow it in prayer, we too can experience the inworking of Christ's excellence.

PRAYING THIS NAME

Using Isaiah's experience, a threefold outline emerges to help us pray in Jesus' name, the Brightness of God's Glory.

First, *come with worship and behold the awesomeness of God.* "I saw the Lord . . . high and lifted up," declared the prophet (Isa. 6:1). The human pursuit of excellence seeks to put forth man's best, but the divine approach to excellence begins with bowing before the Lord.

Further, the full meaning of the Hebrew word *ra-ah*, translated "saw" in this verse, is especially significant. It means to see something with absolute clarity. We must not allow anything to obstruct our vision. To worship God effectively we must have a proper view of Him—but such a view only comes to those who take time to study God's nature and character as revealed in His Word. Those who plunge deepest into God's Word rise highest in their praises of His glory.

Second, *open your heart to the fire of God's purifying promise.* "Woe is me . . . I am a man of unclean lips, and I dwell in the midst of a people of unclean lips," the prophet prayed (Isa. 6:5). The path to excellence is found through casting aside every evil pretension. The real possibility of glory will open only to those who renounce the notion that their flesh can ever attain it. This is accomplished in prayer through the confession of sin. Paul said, "Let us purify ourselves from everything that contaminates body and spirit, perfecting holiness out of reverence for God" (2 Cor. 7:1, NIV).

Finally, *allow God's work to mature you and prepare you for service.* Isaiah not only opened himself to the cleansing fire of God, but he immediately submitted to the commissioning voice of God. "Here am I! Send me," he cries (Isa. 6:8). God may well have a specific mission reserved just for you today. But to receive your marching orders for that mission you'll need a quiet time to saturate yourself in the Brightness of God's Glory, something that is not a feeling but a person—Christ Himself.

So in Jesus' name today we can speak "excellence" into all we do. The student can speak excellence into his studies. The athlete can speak excellence into his sport. The businessman can speak excellence into his business dealings. And the homemaker can speak excellence into managing the activities of her household.

Never again do any of us need to be bound by a second-rate spirit. When we begin to see that Jesus is the Brightness of God's Glory, we will find that praying in Jesus' name opens the way to living in the splendid fullness of all that His person implies.

TODAY'S PRAYER

Dear Lord,
There seem to be so many times I am swallowed up
by the discouraging sense of my own second-ratedness.
I try so hard and do so poorly.
I start so well and end so quickly.
I give it my best and discover it isn't enough.
And so I come to You, the Savior of my soul—
You who have so completely saved me that nothing
of my own failure or sin could restrict the unlimited
power of Your salvation.

Come to me now.
Come in the excellency of the brightness
of Your glorious person and fill my life.
At those points where my own handicap, restrictions, or
mediocrity prevail,
come in the excellence of Your nature and power.
I choose You today.
I receive the resources of Your excellence
as my source, my supply and my shelter.
I both receive and take refuge in Your completeness.

Thank You, Jesus.
My todays can't be mediocre anymore.
Your excellence is beginning to overflow around me.
Amen.

HALLOWING THIS NAME

Chiefest among Ten Thousand—Song of Sol. 5:10
Crown of Glory—Isa. 28:5
Diadem of Beauty—Isa. 28:5
Excellent—Ps. 148:13 (KJV)
Garden of Renown—Ezek. 34:29
Glorious Throne to His Father's House—Isa. 22:23

Glory of Your People Israel—Luke 2:37
Hope of Glory—Col. 1:27
King in His Beauty—Isa. 33:17
King of Glory—Ps. 24:10
My Glory—Ps. 3:3
Polished Shaft—Isa. 49:2
Sign—Luke 2:34
Son of the Most High God—Mark 5:7
Son of Righteousness—Mal. 4:2
Sun and Shield—Ps. 84:11
Wonderful—Isa. 9:6
Your Glorious Sword—Deut. 33:29 (NIV)

11

THE EXPRESS IMAGE
OF HIS PERSON
Hebrews 1:3

REALITY

Defending God's existence, Sir Isaac Newton wrote in *Principia*, "He is not eternity or infinity, but eternal and infinite; He is not duration or space, but He endures and is present. He endures forever and is everywhere present; and by existing always and everywhere, He constitutes duration and space. Since every particle of space is always, and every indivisible moment of duration is everywhere, certainly the Maker and Lord of all things cannot be never and nowhere."[1]

God indeed is somewhere, and those who desire a glimpse of Him need look no further than Jesus. Paul underscored this with his reminder, "As you have therefore received Christ Jesus the Lord, so walk in Him. . . . For in Him dwells all the fullness of the Godhead bodily" (Col. 2:6, 9). And John, in referring to Christ as the Word, clearly equated Christ with God. He wrote, "In the beginning was the Word, and the Word was with God, and *the Word was God!*" (John 1:1, italics added). Just as God is real, so Christ is real—the literal "image of the person of God."

Sadly, some try to argue within themselves against the reality of God—and hence His Son—simply because acknowledging God's existence is the first step toward submitting fully to His rulership. In his *Visions of Heaven and Hell*, John Bunyan said, "When wicked persons have gone on in a course of sin and find they have reason to fear the just judgment of God for their sins, they begin at first to wish that there were no God to punish them; then by degrees they persuade themselves that there is none; and they set themselves to study for arguments to back their opinion."[2]

KNOWING THIS NAME

The author of Hebrews not only introduces us to Christ, the Brightness of God's Glory (as developed in the previous chapter), but also to Christ, the Express Image of His Person (Heb. 1:3).

Of special significance in the text for this lesson is the phrase "who being," which introduces Christ as the Express Image of God's Person. This expression emphasizes the fact that it is Christ's nature simply "to be." He said, "Before Abraham was, I AM" (John 8:58). Christ not only exists, but He cannot be anything other than what He is. And He is all that He is all of the time. It is His nature to always be the things He is being right now; this is no temporary matter.

Consider also the phrase "the express image," which comes from the Greek word *charakter*, meaning "image." It is from this word that we derive our word *character*. This word includes several unique meanings that directly apply to our understanding of Christ, the Express Image of God's Person.

First, *charakter or image describes a mark or stamp that is engraved, etched, branded, cut, or imprinted.* This would include the brand used on a horse or a cow, or an impression on a coin. It is also the word used to describe a stamp embossed on a document.

Second, *this word is used to describe the mark of the Antichrist imprinted on hands or foreheads of his adherents* (Rev. 13:16).

Third, *this is the word used in what is called representative art.* This is art in which a figure or design in a painting or sculpture is meant to represent something that is real in the physical realm. This "image" represents to the viewer what is actually and readily existent in another realm.

When we apply these definitions to Christ, the ramifications are indeed exciting. Jesus came as the physical, actual, and original image of God (the very image God originally intended to be upon man) to re-stamp us with God's image. He, alone, is able to be that "perfect (holy) representative" of the God of the ultimate realm—ultimate meaning eternal (as opposed to temporal) and holy (as opposed to fallen and sinful).

71

Consider the implications this has for you and me! Being "branded" by the stamp of Christ's likeness, we become God's possession once again. As the sheep of His pasture, we carry His brand! The mark of the antichrist spirit of the world won't work on us because we've been stamped with Christ's character forever. Further, like a stamp on an envelope, we have evidence that a certain destiny has been chosen on our behalf. The stamp further proves that the price of our delivery has been paid.

Finally, we must not overlook the significance of the expression of Christ's person. From the Greek word *hupostasis* comes a phrase that means Christ is "the exact stamp of the reality of God the Father and the perfect essence of who the Father literally is."

Hupostasis principally means "something that stands under" and therefore gives a perfect impression of that which is above it. Christ is the sum of all that God is like and about. Beloved, as Jesus stands on earth before mankind He is the perfect impression of the nature and character of God the Father. Christ leaves a full-size stamp; He is the Express Image of God's Person.

LIVING THIS NAME

Through a personal revelation of God's glory, Samuel Morris, whose story is immortalized in the classic *Angel in Ebony*, found Christ in the jungles of Africa. His conversion occurred apart from any direct involvement of a human messenger. Later the Lord directed Samuel to a particular mission compound, where, through the missionary in charge, he learned much more about the Christ He had met in the jungle. Sammy soon learned that God carried out His work on earth through the operations of His "divine agent," the Holy Spirit.

When Sammy asked the missionary how he knew so much about this "Holy Spirit" he explained he had learned about these things at a place called Taylor University, in a land known as the United States of America.

Sammy promptly stood to his feet and asked for directions to this very special place called Taylor University. Amazed at the lad's zeal, the missionary quickly explained that much preparation was needed before making such a journey. For one thing, he explained, it would be necessary for the young man to write Taylor University and request an application for enrollment. Then university administrators would have to evaluate the application and decide if Samuel met the qualifications to enroll as a student.

With the help of the missionary the young convert wrote to the university and waited patiently for his application. Upon its arrival, it was noted by the missionary that the application could not be completed without a picture of the applicant. So Samuel's picture was taken and sent away for processing. Weeks later the first photo the young African had ever seen of himself arrived at the compound. As the missionary placed it in Sammy's hands he was surprised by the youth's insistence that the picture couldn't possibly be of him. Surely someone had made a mistake. When the missionary finally convinced Sammy that the picture indeed was his, the lad simply started to cry. He was certain now that the university would never accept him. With tears streaming down his face, Sammy softly explained, "My picture is too ugly. Oh, that I could send them a picture of Jesus."

But that is precisely what we can do. For when we live in Jesus' name, the Express Image of God's Person, we will conduct the business of our days in such a way that we reflect the beauty of Christ Himself. We will give our world a picture of Jesus wherever we go. And the more of Jesus that floods our being, the clearer the picture of Him will be.

PRAYING THIS NAME

In prayer today God desires to stamp our petitions with the imprint of His Son's reality. He longs to impress the mark of Christ's nature and character into everything we do. As we pray today in Jesus' name, the Express Image of God's Person, we should be careful to concentrate special attention on the first petition Jesus taught us to pray: "Your kingdom come. Your will be done" (Matt. 6:10). To pray "Your kingdom come" in all we do today is to declare God's imprint in every part of our day. It is to proclaim Christ's lordship over family, work, relationships, and even future plans and goals. It is to ask the Lord to mark every moment with the imprint of Jesus' name—our Express Image of God's Person!

TODAY'S PRAYER

Lord, I pray today with the composer who honored You with his song:

O to be like Thee, Blessed Redeemer,
This is my constant longing and prayer;
Gladly I'll forfeit all the earth's treasure,
Jesus Thy perfect likeness to wear.
O to be like Thee, O to be like Thee,
Blessed Redeemer, pure as Thou art.
Come in Thy sweetness,
Come in Thy fullness.
Stamp Thine own image deep on my heart.

Thomas O. Chisholm

HALLOWING THIS NAME

Beginning of the Creation of God—Rev. 3:14
Branch of the Lord—Isa. 4:2
Branch out of His Roots—Isa. 11:1
Chosen of God—Luke 23:35
Emmanuel (God with Us)—Matt. 1:23
Eternally Blessed God—Rom. 9:5
Everlasting Father—Isa. 9:6
Faithful and True—Rev. 19:11
Faithful and True Witness—Rev. 3:14
Faithful Witness—Rev. 1:5
Firstborn among Many Brethren—Rom. 8:29
Firstborn from the Dead—Col. 1:18
Firstborn over all Creation—Col. 1:15
God Manifest in the Flesh—1 Tim. 3:16
His Only Begotten Son—John 3:16
Image of God—2 Cor. 4:4
Image of the Invisible God—Col. 1:15
King's Son—Ps. 72:1
Lord Both of the Dead and the Living—Rom. 14:9
Mighty God—Isa. 9:6
My Elect One—Isa. 42:1
My Lord and My God—John 20:28
Only Begotten of the Father—John 1:14
Root of Jesse—Isa. 11:10
Son of God—John 1:34
Son of the Father—2 John 3
Son of the Highest—Luke 1:32
True God—1 John 5:20
Witness to the People—Isa. 55:4

12

THE PROPITIATION FOR OUR SINS
1 John 2:2

FORGIVENESS

J. Wilbur Chapman told the story of an old woman who stumbled and fell from the top of a stone staircase as she walked from a Boston police station. An officer immediately called for an ambulance and the woman was taken to a nearby hospital where doctors held out little hope for her recovery.

"She'll not live a day," a physician told an attending nurse. Concerned, the nurse befriended the dying woman and in a few hours had won her confidence.

Motioning for the nurse to come near, the old woman said sorrowfully, "I have traveled all the way from California by myself, stopping at every city of importance between San Francisco and Boston. In each city I visit just two places: the police station and the hospital. You see, my boy ran away from home and I have no idea where he is. I've got to find him. So I've sold all my possessions and made this journey, somehow hoping for a miracle."

The mother's eyes seemed to flash a ray of hope as she added, "Someday he may even come into this very hospital, and if he does, please promise me you'll tell him his two best friends never gave up on him."

With that the doctor drew near and quietly told the nurse, "She'll be gone in a matter of minutes. There's nothing we can do."

Bending over the dying mother, the nurse whispered softly, "Tell me the names of those two friends so I can tell your son if I ever see him."

With trembling lips and her eyes filled with tears the mother responded, "Tell him those two friends were God and his mother," and she closed her eyes and died.

God, even more than a forgiving mother, never gives up on one of His children. His forgiveness is uniquely infinite. It is infinite in that it is never-ending; it is unique to the degree that it is one of a kind. Who else in the universe can genuinely forgive and at the same time forget? (See Heb. 8:12.) And since God is the quintessence of forgiveness, to think on God is to immerse oneself in thoughts of forgiveness rather than failure. As Søren Kierkegaard suggests, "When the thought of God does not remind a man of his sin but that he is forgiven, and the past is no longer the memory of how much he did wrong but of how much he was forgiven—then that man rests in the forgiveness of his sins."[1] Elsewhere in his *Journals* Kierkegaard wrote, "God creates out of nothing. 'Wonderful,' you say. Yes, to be sure, but He does what is even more wonderful: He makes saints out of sinners."[2]

KNOWING THIS NAME

John helps us understand this concept of God's capacity to cover our sins (and thus forget them) by referring to Christ as the Propitiation for Our Sins (1 John 2:2). Concerning the English origins of the somewhat uncommon word *propitiation,* it is interesting to note its relationship to the rather common word *prop,* which is something that supports, sustains, or strengthens. Further, when a person needing support receives it at a timely moment and in a favorable or encouraging manner, it is said to be "propitious," meaning to "favorably incline the circumstance or to increase the likelihood of acceptable results."

Jesus Christ has become our Propitiator—one who has favorably inclined our circumstance toward God. To propitiate on our behalf Jesus gave Himself. He shed His blood, and so His life in its perfect essence was poured out to give God a favorable disposition toward us.

The New Testament Greek word for propitiation, *hilasterion,* means "that which expiates, atones, or returns a favor." It was used in the ancient world of "votive offerings" (offerings given to fulfill certain vows of dedication). When used in reference to Christ it means our Lord unconditionally fulfilled His vow to provide the way for us to come back to God. Further, Jesus unconditionally fulfilled any perceived obligation on our part that was necessary for us to gain acceptance before God.

Many people make the mistake of thinking it is necessary to negotiate with God in order to be accepted by Him. They sometimes pray, "Lord, I'll do this for You if You'll do that for me." But as the Propitiator for Our Sins, Christ has done *everything* necessary to fulfill any vow we could make to "better ourselves" in God's eyes. On these terms we can come to God freely, knowing we are forgiven by Him fully. What a joyous reality!

Interestingly, the same Greek word (*hilasterion*) is translated in 1 John 2:2 as "propitiation" and in Hebrews 9:3 as "mercy seat." "Mercy seat" refers to the cover or lid placed on the Ark of the Covenant in the Holy of Holies. Even the Septuagint translation of the Old Testament, which was the Hebrew translated into the Greek, uses the word *hilasterion* when referring to the mercy seat in tabernacle worship (see Exod. 25:22).

This is significant because the mercy seat is where the blood of the sacrificial lamb was poured on the Day of Atonement. Annually, when all the sins of the people were dealt with, the high priest entered into the Holy of Holies to pour the blood onto the *hilasterion* or mercy seat. Equally interesting is that, within the Ark, just below the mercy seat, lay God's Law (the Ten Commandments) that man had broken. But now the blood of a blameless substitute, resting upon the mercy seat, is interposed between God and His broken law.

What a powerful picture of Christ. As our sinless substitute Jesus poured out His life on the cross as a propitiation before God. He comes between God's requirements for perfection and purity and our imperfection and impurity. Since Jesus is absolutely perfect, God sees the record of His sinless life instead of our sin and is disposed to accept us completely. We are "seated" in Christ (Eph. 2:6), and thereby receive God's mercy and forgiveness.

LIVING THIS NAME

"Cover me!" a soldier cries to his fellow troops in the heat of battle as he prepares to rush into the conflict. He's asking his companions to provide artillery while he advances against the enemy. So

Jesus is our covering as we move into each day's warfare. And He serves as this covering in more ways than one. Not only does He "cover" in the sense of providing artillery against the enemy, but Christ's blood is the literal covering for all our sins and failures. There's never a failure that can reach beyond God's ability to forgive. Phillips Brooks in *Perennials* said, "It will not do for any of us to make up his mind that he cannot be any good nor do any noble thing, until first he has asked himself whether it is as impossible in God's sight as in his."[3]

Beloved, to live today in Jesus' name is not only to recognize Christ as our Propitiator, but to take the quality of that spirit into our relationships with others. Just as Jesus covers and cleanses our sins with His blood (1 John 1:9), we need to cover the failures of others with our love (Prov. 10:12). We need to allow a spirit of forgiveness to flood us. Remember when Peter asked Christ if it was enough to forgive a transgression seven times, He responded, "Seventy times seven!" (Matt. 18:21-22).

PRAYING THIS NAME

To pray in Jesus' name, the Propitiator for Our Sins, is to pray in the totality of Christ's unconditional forgiveness. At the heart of the pattern prayer Christ taught His disciples is the petition "Forgive us our debts, as we forgive our debtors" (Matt. 6:12). The idea of debts here is not so much a reference to money owed as to a "sin debt" owed. In fact, one paraphrase of this verse reads, "Forgive us our sins, just as we have forgiven those who have sinned against us" (TLB).

If Jesus' name means forgiveness, an idea clearly conveyed by the word *propitiation*, then praying in Jesus' name means we are praying in the fullness of His forgiveness. We are speaking His forgiveness into situations that we anticipate might minimize a day's potential. If, for example, a brother has wronged you, speak forgiveness into that situation. And if God should impress on your heart (as He often will) to go directly to that brother with a word of forgiveness, you should cover that encounter with prayer even before it actually happens.

And above all, in praying today fervently seek to place every transgression under the "blood covering" of Christ who, alone, is the Propitiator for Our Sins. May we deal as decisively with each sin as did John Wesley when he prayed:

Forgive them all, O Lord:
Our sins of omission and our sins of commission;
The sins of our youth and the sins of our riper years;
The sins of our souls and the sins of our bodies;
Our secret and our more open sins;
Our sins of ignorance and surprise,
And our more deliberate and presumptuous sins;
The sins we have done to please ourselves,
And the sins we have done to please others;
The sins we know and remember, and the sins we have
forgotten;
The sins we have striven to hide from others,
And the sins by which we have made others offend.
Forgive them, O Lord, forgive them all for His sake,
Who died for our sins and rose for our justification,
And now stands at Thy right hand to make intercession
For us,
Jesus Christ our Lord.[4]

TODAY'S PRAYER

Father,
I bow today with a renewed sense of gratitude
for Your all-encompassing provision in Jesus.
It is so mightily assuring to be reminded from Your Word that
my debt of sin is completely paid;
my broken past completely forgiven;
my list of failures completely destroyed;
my record of disobedience completely forgotten.
Please accept my prayer, my confession,
that I sometimes am overcome by the cloud of
condemnation cast upon me by my adversary.

Today, Lord,
I rise with the banner of the blood of Jesus,
to hurl it in the adversary's face.
In Jesus' name, my propitiation is complete;
my sin is completely covered;
I am completely free.

I rise to walk into this day,
and all of my tomorrows,

circled by the Savior's righteousness,
clothed in Jesus' sinless excellence,
rejoicing in my full acceptance.
Thank You, Lord!
In Jesus' name.
Amen.

HALLOWING THIS NAME

Advocate—1 John 2:1
Apostle and High Priest—Heb. 3:1
Author of Eternal Salvation—Heb. 5:9
Father of Mercies—2 Cor. 1:3
Forerunner—Heb. 6:20
God of All Grace—1 Pet. 5:10
God of Recompense—Jer. 51:56
Great High Priest—Heb. 4:14
Habitation of Justice—Jer. 50:7
Hope of Glory—Col. 1:27
Indescribable Gift—2 Cor. 9:15
Jehovah-Tsidkenu (The Lord Our Righteousness)—Jer. 23:6; 33:16
King of Righteousness—Heb. 7:2
Lamb in the Midst of the Throne—Rev. 5:6
Lamb Slain—Rev. 3:18
Lord, Your Redeemer—Isa. 43:14
Mediator—Job 9:33; 1 Tim. 2:5
Mediator of a Better Covenant—Heb. 8:6
My Elect One—Isa. 42:1
My Salvation—Ps. 38:22
Our Passover—1 Cor. 5:7
Tower of Salvation—2 Sam. 22:51
Unspeakable Gift—2 Cor. 9:15 (KJV)

13

THE HIDDEN MANNA
Revelation 2:17

PROVISION

Days were difficult for the young couple as they sat down to eat
the barest of meals. Each had but a hamburger patty and a glass
of milk. The husband's college bills had piled up and neither had
been able to find work. Their last few dollars were spent that
morning at a nearby market to purchase the milk and meat.

With his voice cracking, the young husband offered thanks,
wondering if saying grace was even in order since they had so
little. After stuttering through a brief thank you the husband
added a simple petition: "Lord, we're not asking for much, just
enough to get by—and this is hardly enough." With tears in his
eyes he added, "At least, Lord, give us the staples we need to go
with what little we have. That's all we ask for Lord, just the
staples!"

As they began to eat their modest meal the husband winced
with sudden pain. He had bitten into a sharp object that was
hidden in the meat. Fishing the object from his mouth, he stared
in amazement at a small metal staple that had been in the meat.
Both husband and wife began laughing as the husband joked,
"That's not what I meant, Lord!"

Neither, of course, was able to finish the meal for fear of finding
more staples, so the husband promptly headed back to the market

with the uneaten patties in hand. The young couple was concerned that others might encounter the same problem and possibly experience a serious injury.

Naturally the store manager was deeply worried, and, although the young husband made no threats at taking legal action, the manager immediately sought to make amends. "Sir," the manager blurted out, "if you'll be so kind as to forget this ever happened, you can fill up one of those shopping carts with all the groceries you can use for a week. They'll be on the house!"

KNOWING THIS NAME

Wherever we are this moment, chances are as we look about, we can see testimony of God's promise to provide—staples and all. In our homes are furniture, clothing, and the like. When we sit in a park or in some outside setting we see the marvelous provisions of nature in the trees, the flowers, the birds singing continual praises to our Lord. Have we failed to recognize these details of life as blessings God designed specifically for His children? Henry Ward Beecher observed, "So many are God's kindnesses to us that, as drops of water, they run together; and it is not until we are born up by the multitude of them, as by streams in deep channels, that we recognize them as coming from Him."[1]

We are too often unaware of the many hidden pleasures of God within hand's reach. The air we have just breathed, the lungs into which that air has flowed, and the capacity of the body to transform that air into fuel to further life are all gracious gifts from God. Infinite indeed are His abundant provisions to His people, including the best of all His blessings: His very presence. Alfred Lord Tennyson said poetically in *The Higher Pantheism:*

> Speak to Him thou for He hears, and Spirit
> with Spirit can meet—
> Closer is He than breathing, and nearer
> than hands and feet.

Christ's presence is clearly our provision for all we need, our Hidden Manna for surviving life's journey. In our text for this title, Revelation 2:17, Christ says, "To him who overcomes I will give some of the hidden manna to eat." But we know Jesus is referring to Himself because of His earlier words in John 6:31-35. It is here that Christ describes Himself as the Manna that came down from heaven, referring back to the early example of miraculous provision during Israel's wilderness sojourn. He is telling us that He is the final fulfillment of that provision.

We first discover this forty-year-long miracle of provision in Exodus 16. Later, in Joshua 5:11-12 we read of the conclusion of this unusual six-day-per-week, fifty-two-weeks-per-year miracle. Scripture says, "They ate of the produce of the land on the day after the Passover, unleavened bread and parched grain on the very same day. *Now the manna ceased on the day after they had eaten the produce of the land;* and the children of Israel no longer had manna, but they ate the food of the land of Canaan that year" (Josh. 5:11-12; italics added).

To understand the significance of the title "the Hidden Manna," consider the context in which we find it: Rev. 2:12-17. This section of Scripture features Christ's letter written to correct the compromising church of Pergamos. The church's impurity came from eating "things sacrificed to idols" (verse 14). In other words, they were guilty of a worldly diet that led to excessive indulgence in other important aspects of life.

A vital lesson emerges: When we depend on human resources for our provision, or worse yet, compromise our faith to insure our personal or financial security, we open the door to ever-broadening dimensions of failure. Christ wants us to depend on Him, and only Him, for sufficiency. The Father's guarantee of provision is to be our only grounds for security, whether material or physical.

Enhancing this thought is the importance of the word *hidden.* This is a specific reference to the command God gave to Moses, telling him that a vessel of manna should be placed in the Ark of the Covenant "to be kept for your generations" (Exod. 16:32-34). The Ark of the Covenant was lost to history, disappearing from its place in the temple. Archaeologists have not been able to find it, though they've sought it for many centuries. Surely God removed it in order for us to focus more clearly on the one who is the true fulfillment of all the Ark represented—Christ Himself. "In Christ" we have the fulfillment of provision, of the manna that was sealed away until a future day. And all who have acknowledged Christ's lordship have prospered in this provision.

LIVING THIS NAME

Living today in Christ, our Hidden Manna, is to live in a recognition that he, alone, is our "secret provision" for all we need. This reality is beautifully exemplified in various case studies in Scripture—most notably in the Old Testament account we've already mentioned. Recall how this miracle supply always came in unexplained ways. ("Manna," in fact, literally means "What is it?") Further, the manna always arrived at a time when no one could do anything about it—during the night as the Israelites slept.

Even in this latter thought we find a unique hidden insight. Perhaps when God says, "I'll provide for you," He expects us to rest and let Him take care of the providing. We shouldn't be too surprised if His provisions come during life's "nighttime" experiences—those occasions when things seem to be at their darkest. So, though we may not be able to see tomorrow for the darkness, God is already at work preparing tomorrow's provision today!

Consider also God's special provision for Elijah (1 Kings 17:1-7). Faced with famine on every side, while in exile out of fear for his life, Elijah was visited twice daily by ravens, God's appointed "manna messengers," who fed the prophet bread and meat. When the Lord provides "hidden manna," there is no place too difficult or too lonely for Him to work, neither is there any means too unlikely (remember those ravens and the "staples") for Him to use. He will meet our needs.

PRAYING THIS NAME

Another glorious biblical example of God's "manna provision" is discovered in the experience of King Jehoiachin upon his release from prison (2 Kings 25:27).

Jehoiachin, King of Judah, had been in prison for thirty-seven years during Judah's Babylonian captivity when Evil-merodach, king of Babylon, issued his pardon. But he did more than merely release Jehoiachin. He actually elevated him to a position of leadership above all the other kings who were in Babylon. And, according to the account, Evil-merodach changed Jehoiachin's prison garments, and he ate bread "continually all the days of his life." The lesson concludes with this beautiful testimony: "And as for his provisions, there was a regular ration given him by the king, a portion for each day, all the days of his life" (2 Kings 25:30).

To pray today in Jesus' name, our Hidden Manna, is to pray in the recognition that Christ is capable of providing for our every need. It is to trust that our provision will be a "continual portion" given by the King Himself at a "daily rate" for all the days of our lives. It is to pray with new confidence the literal translation of that petition of the Lord's prayer, "Give us this day our daily bread."

Ignatius Loyola was the youngest of eleven children. He grew up in Spain centuries ago and he surely understood Christ to be the Hidden Manna. In his forty-third year, an age considered well-advanced by sixteenth-century standards, Loyola took an enormous step of faith that involved the surrender of all his wealth and worldly claims. Having moved to Paris, Ignatius gathered six disciples around him to establish a new order called "The Company of Jesus," or Jesuits. Incredibly, just twenty-two years later at Loyola's death in 1556, those half-dozen disciples had grown to one thousand, many of whom—like Francis Xavier who visited fifty-two nations in just ten years—had gone to the ends of the earth as foreign missionaries. But most significant is the fact that Ignatius Loyola trusted God implicitly. As he neared life's end, Loyola prayed with passion:

> Take, Lord, all my liberty,
> my memory, my understanding,
> and my whole being.
> You have given me all that I have,
> all that I am,
> and I surrender all to Your divine will,
> that You dispose of me.
> Give me only Your love and Your grace,
> with this I am rich enough,
> and I have no more to ask.[2]

TODAY'S PRAYER

Bread of heaven, sent to earth below
To fill the starving heart of man
Midst the famine of this worldly scene;
Thou art welcome to my soul.

Bread of heaven, broken once for all,
That none must go unfed today.

Broken Manna giv'n to weary souls,
Come, O man, and freely dine.

Bread of heaven, blest Redeemer,
I'll feast on Thy provision;
Thus I'll walk and never languish,
Having fed on Thy supply.

Bread of heaven, soon-returning Lord,
I'll watch for heaven's rending,
But until then I will occupy,
Strengthened by Thy life within.

Bread of heaven, Jesus Christ my Lord,
Thou art my soul's supply.
Come and feed me, blessed Savior,
Come and fill, for Thou hast promised
Hungry souls to satisfy.

J.W.H.

HALLOWING THIS NAME
As Rivers of Water in a Dry Place—Isa. 32:2
Bread of Life—John 6:35
Garden of Renown—Ezek. 34:29
Gift of God—John 4:10
Grain Offering—Lev. 2:1-10
Grain of Wheat—John 12:23-24
Heir of All Things—Heb. 1:2
Jehovah-Jireh (The Lord Will Provide)—Gen. 22:8-14
Living Bread—John 6:51
Manna—Exod. 16:31
My Portion—Pss. 73:26; 119:57
Offering—Eph. 5:2
Our Passover—1 Cor. 5:7
Portion of Jacob—Jer. 51:19
Portion of My Inheritance—Ps. 16:5
Rain upon the Mown Grass—Ps. 72:6
Rewarder—Heb. 11:6
Strength to the Poor and Needy—Isa. 25:4
True Bread from Heaven—John 6:32
Your Exceedingly Great Reward—Gen. 15:1

THE AMEN
Revelation 3:14

FINALITY

When asked to comment on his personal practices in prayer, Martin Luther responded, "I give you the best I have; I tell you how I myself pray. May our Lord grant you to do better." Then, following a few moments instruction, Luther concluded, "And finally . . . mark this! Make your 'amen' strong, never doubting that God is surely listening to you. This is what 'amen' means. It means that I know with certainty that my prayer has been heard by God."[1]

Martin Luther was emphasizing that a bold "amen" was a statement of confirmation. It was an indication that the person praying truly believed his prayers would be answered. Because *amen* means "it is done," or "let it be so," to make this assertion boldly, according to Luther, was to declare with confidence that so far as the petition was concerned, the matter in question was settled by the petitioner's prayer.

"Amen" is another title ascribed to our Lord in Scripture (Rev. 3:14). Jesus Christ is our eternal "It Is Done!" His very name speaks finality to every assault by Satan. In a certain sense, Jesus' name might be likened to the very signature of God appearing on the bottom line of every claim we make. As Joseph Parker suggests in his *Sermons*, "Everywhere I find the signature, the autograph of God, and He will never deny His own handwriting.

God hath set His tabernacle in the dewdrop as surely as in the sun. No man can any more create the smallest flower than He could create the greatest world."[2]

Make no mistake about it: God's signature over all creation is His Son, for it was by Him (Christ) that all things were created (Col. 1:16; John 1:3). Christ, indeed, is God's divine "Let it be so!"

KNOWING THIS NAME

A description of our Lord, the Amen, is found in Revelation 3:14. We read: "These are the words of the Amen, the faithful and true witness, the ruler of God's creation" (NIV). As is the case with so many passages of Scripture that describe titles of our Lord, this verse pictures three distinct expressions of Christ's person: the Amen, the faithful and true witness, and the ruler of God's creation. For now, we'll concentrate primarily on the first expression—the Amen.

The word *amen* occurs seventy-eight times in the Bible: twenty-seven times in the Old Testament and fifty-one times in the New. Upon further study, it may seem peculiar for many that when concluding a prayer with the expression "in Jesus' name, Amen," we are in fact declaring both Jesus' name (Jesus) and one of His titles (Amen). It is almost as if we were saying, "in Jesus' name, Jesus!"

Sadly, the word *amen* is so common in our liturgical and devotional usage that it sometimes loses its intended meaning. But to discover that saying "amen" can be the same as saying "Jesus" presents us with a profoundly significant fact.

As suggested, the basic meaning of *amen* is "let it be so," or, "it is done." But this expresses far more than merely a passing wish, as if one were praying, "Oh, I hope what I have prayed really happens!" The actual force of the word *amen* is best seen in its translation into the Septuagint version of the Old Testament. When Jewish scholars translated the Old Testament Hebrew word for *amen* into what they conceived to be the Greek equivalency, they used the Greek word *genoito*. The literal translation of this is "Let this come into being; let it exist."

In other words, when we declare "amen" in prayer, we invoke God's creative power, and that is far more significant than a mere utterance of wishful thinking.

LIVING THIS NAME

To live today in Jesus' name, then, is to declare over the day, "God bring these things into being." As our Amen, Christ is the final authority on any situation or circumstance we may encounter. Christ alone establishes, secures, settles, and fixes the Father's will in each moment we live. It is His responsibility to put God's will in place, and He does so wherever people pray, "Thy kingdom come, Thy will be done . . . in Jesus' name, Amen."

To live in the certainty of Christ, our Amen—whom John calls the Word (John 1:1)—brings to mind Peter's statement in 2 Peter 1:19: "We have the prophetic Word made more sure." In this context, Peter is discussing the trustworthiness of God's Word given to us by His Holy Spirit. What a contrast to the shifting, deceptive words and trends of mere human origin. The Greek word for "sure," *bebaioteron,* is a strong term stressing the firmness, strength, and unshakable reality of the "more sure Word" God has given us. Thus His promises given in Christ are both assured to us as unshakably true and available to us ultimately, conclusively, and with final certainty. In Jesus' name, our Amen, our sure "Word" is firmly secured. Our "So Be It" says so!

Further, when we refer to the Amen as reflective of Christ's finality, it becomes more than merely a concluding term to a prayer. It becomes the declaration that in the end Christ's power will determine the outcome of every situation we face. We must live each moment in His "Amen power." literally His power to create. And since in His name there is an unlimited supply of this power, nothing in accordance with His will (1 John 5:14) can be hindered from being brought into reality.

This truth is further underscored by Paul's words in 2 Corinthians, "For no matter how many promises God has made, they are 'yes' in Christ. And so through Him the 'amen' is spoken by us to the glory of God" (1:20, NIV).

PRAYING THIS NAME

When we apply this understanding of the Amen to personal prayer, a thrilling truth emerges: *Every promise of God is imparted in the person of Christ Himself.* And because Jesus is the "Incarnate Word," when we pray in His name He becomes to us the "Confirming Word." Every promise we claim today in prayer is "amened" in Christ by God.

Think of it in these terms: Today as you claim a promise concerning a specific need and then declare that need in Jesus' name, it is as though the Father Himself says, "Amen . . . let the promise I have given now be fulfilled for the glory of My Son!"

Finally, when praying today in Jesus' name, our Amen, we would do well to remember the context in which this title of Christ appears. It is found in Revelation 3:14, in a letter addressed to the church at Laodicea where people are being lulled by the idea that their own resources are sufficient for their many needs. We hear them testifying that they "are rich, have become wealthy, and have need of nothing" (Rev. 3:17). The Lord, however, declares that the Laodicean church is impoverished, despite their appearance of wealth.

The message is abundantly clear: The final estimate of our worth is not what we have in our hands but what our Creator has to say. Thus, a person in prayer with the Amen on his lips is in a better overall position than a person with a checkbook and large bank account who is standing in line at his bank. The latter's resource is temporal. The former, eternal. So, praying in Jesus' name, the Amen, is praying with the recognition that Christ alone is the final authority in all those matters for which we are praying. It is offering our petitions with the awareness that, as far as Christ is concerned, what we have claimed today in accordance with God's will is final. Christ's name assures it. God's sovereignty "amens" it. Therefore, it is done!

TODAY'S PRAYER

As you come to prayer today, select various promises from God's Word that apply to specific needs you might have. Here are some examples:

Lord,
I come with high praises to You
because You have given me Your Word,
and Your Word is true.
I come to stand *upon* Your Word,
and to live *within* the person of Jesus, the Amen.

In Jesus' name I say, "Amen," to Your promises:
"All things work together for good. . . ."
"You will supply all my need. . . ."
"You are the Lord who heals. . . ."
"You are not willing that any should perish. . . ."
"You are able to redeem me from the hand of the wicked. . . ."
Because You have spoken Your Word,
because You have settled it in heaven, and
because You have given it to me—
I say, "Amen!"

And in saying "amen," I step within the circumference
of my Lord Jesus' circle of power and grace,
knowing that
He is Your Word Incarnate.
All Your promises are verified in Him, and
I am living today in Him . . . and in those promises.
Thank You, Father.
In Jesus' name.
Amen!

HALLOWING THIS NAME

Beginning of the Creation of God—Rev. 3:14
Chief Cornerstone—Ps. 118:22
Faithful and True—Rev. 19:11
Finisher of Our Faith—Heb. 12:2
First and the Last—Rev. 1:17
God of Truth—Deut. 32:4
God the Judge of All—Heb. 12:23
I Am—John 8:58
Judge and Lawgiver—Isa. 33:22
Lord God of Truth—Ps. 31:5
Lord of All—Acts 10:36
Lord of All the Earth—Zech. 6:5
Lord over All—Rom. 10:12
Man Attested by God—Acts 2:22
Mighty One of Israel—Isa. 30:29
Strength to the Needy—Isa. 25:4
Upholder of All Things—Heb. 1:3

15

THE LION OF THE TRIBE OF JUDAH
Revelation 5:5

BOLDNESS

"Pray the largest prayers," preached Phillips Brooks. "You cannot think of a prayer so large that God, in answering it, will not wish you had made it larger. Pray not for crutches—pray for wings!"[1]

We've been instructed by our Lord to come boldly to His throne of grace (Heb. 4:16), and this boldness is wrapped up in Jesus' name, the Lion of the Tribe of Judah (Rev. 5:5).

KNOWING THIS NAME

Boldness, bathed in audacity and tempered by tenacity, is foundational to fruitful living and praying in Jesus' name. We need an audacity like that of the newly converted teenager who was asked by his pastor if the Devil ever tried to tell him he wasn't really born again.

"Yes, sometimes," the youth answered.

"Well, how do you respond?" queried the pastor.

"I tell him it's none of his business whether I'm a Christian or not."

Such boldness, beloved, is a valued quality of Christian maturity. A quality that we can discover in the name of Jesus. Boldness is a quality that is particularly embodied in the title John ascribes to Jesus: The Lion of the Tribe of Judah. In Revelation 5:5 we read,

"But one of the elders said to me, 'Do not weep. Behold, the Lion of the tribe of Judah, the Root of David, has prevailed to open the scroll and to loose its seven seals' " (Rev. 5:5).

The context of this verse depicts Christ in His present place of ministry. This is not the picture of the future, it is now! Christ is receiving worship now (Rev. 5:9-14), and He is receiving the prayers of His people now (v. 8). The scroll He takes (5:7) is the "title deed" to this planet. It is an expression of the fact that "all authority in heaven and in earth" has been given to Him (Matt. 28:18).

It is as the Lion of the Tribe of Judah that Christ has gained this position. He is the fountainhead of our boldness. Because Christ possesses all authority, there is no realm of request concerning anything in heaven (the invisible realm of activity) or on earth (the physical, personal, material, or even political realm of activity) that is beyond our privilege. It is ours in Jesus' name, the Lion of the Tribe of Judah.

LIVING THIS NAME

To live effectively in Jesus' name, the Lion of the Tribe of Judah, we must recognize that Christ's power as the Lion results from His work as the Lamb (Rev. 5:6). His authority over the works of hell as well as the kingdoms of earth flows from the Cross (Col. 2:14-15). Through the Cross and the resurrection Christ becomes the fulfillment of Jacob's prophecy over his son Judah, given eighteen hundred years earlier (see Gen. 49:8-12). In Genesis Judah is likened to a lion that springs forth upon its prey, exactly as Christ came forth from the tomb carrying the keys of death and hell (Rev. 1:18).

When Jacob spoke this prophecy he declared, "The scepter shall not depart from Judah . . . until Shiloh comes . . . " (Gen. 49:10). "Shiloh" is a reference to the coming Messiah, and Jacob's promise to Judah is that the rod of authority would be carried by Judah until it would be transferred to the Messiah's hand. As the Lion of Judah, Jesus is the fulfillment of the prophecy in Genesis 49:9: "He has burst forth from the grave like a lion springing upon its prey" (personal paraphrase), which in Christ's case refers to His springing upon all the works of hell.

John writes, "For this purpose the Son of God was manifested, that He might destroy the works of the devil" (1 John 3:8). By His triumph Christ holds the scepter of authority and provides us grounds for being bold in all we do.

Interestingly, the word *destroy* used in 1 John 3:8 is the same Greek word, *luo*, translated "loose" in Matthew 16:19: "Whatever you loose on earth shall be loosed in heaven!" This suggests that our boldness in Christ leads to a ministry of both binding and loosing, all of which focuses on restraining Satan's forces wherever they operate.

So to live today in the recognition that Jesus is the Lion of the Tribe of Judah is to appropriate His boldness as our boldness. Just as Christ burst forth from the grave like a Lion springing upon its prey, He will burst upon every difficult circumstance we might encounter. And in the same sense that a good loud roar from a lion frightens away its enemies, a firm "in Jesus' name" spoken boldly over a troubling situation will loose something of Christ's power into that situation.

PRAYING THIS NAME

It is not without significance that Judah's name means "praise" (Gen. 29:35). When Israel went into battle, Judah, the largest of Israel's tribes, was at the forefront bearing their standard (or "banner") before the entire host of Israel (Num. 2:9; 10:14).

This seems to suggest that the best way to apply the power of Christ's name, the Lion of the Tribe of Judah, is through praise. Just as Judah went into the battle first, so we should begin each day's time of prayer with praise. Indeed, Scripture often links worship and warfare, as we see in the psalmist's words: "Let the high praises of God be in their mouth, and a two-edged sword in their hand" (Ps. 149:6).

When we move into today's battles with praise, the enemy becomes confused and scattered (see 2 Chron. 20:20-23). We quickly discover that whatever burden we may be carrying is lightened by a spirit of rejoicing in the confidence of Christ's victory. As the old camp meeting chorus declares,

> The Lion of Judah
> shall break every chain,
> and give us the victory
> again and again!

Praise, indeed, is essential to victorious prayer. And the more we recognize who God is (which results from increased praises of Him) the more we recognize how insignificant Satan is.

As we pray today we must never forget that our adversary "walks about like a roaring lion, seeking whom he may devour" (1 Pet. 5:8). But even more important, we must remember he has a worthy opponent in another "lion": Christ, the Lion of Judah. No wonder the following verse (5:9) calls for us to stand against the devil in total confidence: "Resist him, standing firm in the faith, because you know that your brothers throughout the world are undergoing the same kind of sufferings" (1 Pet. 5:9, NIV).

We must also remember that our praises of God are directly related to our knowledge of God, and that knowledge comes from a study of His Word. Jesus, for example, repeatedly confronted Satan in the wilderness with the expression, "It is written, . . ." followed by just the right words to repel His adversary (Matt. 4:4). Christ knew what word to use because as a child He had grown in His knowledge of the Law of God. And so it is with our praises. Depth in God's Word means depth in praise, and depth in praise results in victorious warfare.

So explore God's Word today, searching out new ways to praise and worship Christ, the Lion of the Tribe of Judah. The boldness to break the bonds of the evil one is but a breath of worship away. Let's pause even now and begin to praise our way (and our day) to victory.

TODAY'S PRAYER

Hallelujah, Father!
I stand before Your Throne with praise!
Like a banner spread by an advancing troop
going forward in battle, I lift my praises.
Jesus, You are mighty!
Lord God, You are victorious!

Spirit of God, like an all-consuming flame,
go before me and cast down all that oppose
the Father's purpose for my life.

Lord, I am reminded today that You are Jehovah Sabaoth:
The Lord of Hosts.

As the Leader of the troops of heaven,
go before me, O Lord.
As the Lion of the Tribe of Judah,
sweep into battle and vanquish
all the works of darkness that seek to
oppress me,
afflict me,
or destroy me.

I take my position in the resources of Jesus' name.
While You battle on my behalf,
I bow to praise Your mighty name.
Hallelujah, Father!
In Christ I am more than a conqueror.
In Jesus' name.
Amen.

HALLOWING THIS NAME

Arm of the Lord—Isa. 51:9-10
Author of Our Faith—Heb. 12:2
Commander—Isa. 55:4
Commander of the Army of the Lord—Josh. 5:14
Deliverer—Rom. 11:26
King over All the Earth—Zech. 14:9
Lord Mighty in Battle—Ps. 24:8
Lord Strong and Mighty—Ps. 24:8
Man of War—Exod. 15:3
Mighty God—Ps. 89:8; Isa. 9:6
Mighty One—Ps. 45:3
My Strength—2 Sam. 22:23
One Who Shall Have Dominion—Num. 24:19
Prophet of the Highest—Luke 1:76
Shield—2 Sam. 22:31
Strong Lord—Ps. 89:8
Sword of Your Excellency—Deut. 33:29
Trap and a Snare—Isa. 8:14
Your Confidence—Prov. 3:26

16
THE ALPHA AND OMEGA
Revelation 1:8

TOTALITY

"All that exists," wrote Francois Fenelon in *Maximes des Saints*, "exists only by the communication of God's infinite being. All that has intelligence, has it only by derivation from His sovereign reason; and all that acts, acts only from the impulse from His supreme activity." The seventeenth-century mystic concludes, "It is He who does all in all; it is He who, at each instant of our life, is the beating of our heart, the movement of our limbs, the light of our eyes, the intelligence of our spirit, the soul of our soul."[1]

Here we have a picture of Christ, the Alpha and Omega, the totality of all we are and ever hope to be. He, alone, is the fullness of God's total revelation to man. And without this revelation mankind has no hope. As Søren Kierkegaard advised, "It is so impossible for the world to exist without God, that if God should forget it, it would immediately cease to be."[2]

KNOWING THIS NAME

Of all that Jesus is, we could say He is as much the Alpha and Omega (Rev. 1:8) as anything else. Christ has always been, and shall ever be, all in all.

This familiar phrase, "the Alpha and Omega," is so frequently quoted that some of its significance tends to be lost. It occurs four times in John's Revelation and each time refers to Christ's totality as a direct revelation of God Himself. It is the one expression of Christ's nature that Christ Himself gave. He said, "I am the Alpha and the Omega, the Beginning and the End. . . ."

The Book of Revelation begins with two references to this title (1:8, 11) and concludes with two of the same (21:6; 22:13). It is as if these declarations are placed by God as weighty "bookends" at the opening and closing of John's Revelation of Christ and His triumph.

In Revelation 1:8 we note the emphasis is on Christ's eternity, that His essence embraces all of time: "I am . . . the Beginning and the End."

In Revelation 1:11 the emphasis shifts to Christ's lordship: "I am . . . the First and the Last." Here Christ is declared to be the head of the church who reigns among His people.

Finally, in Revelation 21:6-7 and 22:12-13, the emphasis is upon His reward. After all that can be removed is removed, Christ remains, wiping away tears, making all things new, giving from the fountain of the water of life to any who is thirsty (Rev. 21:4-6), and rewarding each person according to his work (Rev. 22:12-13).

Note the apostle's detailed unveiling of the features of Christ in Revelation 1:13-16. Each of the various traits described here is referred to in the following two chapters of Revelation as indicative of Christ's capacity to deal effectively with the needs or failures in the churches He addressed. These features include the full-length garment Christ wears (Rev. 1:13), which illustrates both His majesty and authority; the white, snowy hair and fiery eyes (Rev. 1:14), which depict His wisdom and knowledge; the brassy feet and resounding voice (Rev. 1:15), which represent His dominion and rulership; His hands (1:16), which hold church leadership and attend to the churches' ministry; and the characteristics shown in verses 13 and 20 where Christ stands in the midst of the seven candlesticks (symbolic of the seven churches) and holds the seven stars (picturing church leadership in a sustaining, controlling role).

In short, Christ is the totality of power in our world, as carried out through His people. From start to finish, almightiness and all-loveliness are His. He rules and loves through His people—and He wants to unveil all of Himself to them.

The reality of Christ's totality is further underscored in an analysis of the words *alpha* and *omega* as they appear in the Greek language. Of course, these are the first and last letters of the Greek alphabet and as such represent Christ as the beginning and the ending. But consider this direct quote from the Greek lexicon (Bauer, Arndt, Gingrich): "As a symbolic letter the Greek 'a' (alpha) signifies the beginning; the 'o' (omega) the end. The two came to designate the universe and every kind of divine and demonic power." In Jesus' name, then, our Alpha and Omega, exists all power in the universe. He existed before any other power (including demonic) and will continue after all such powers have been subdued.

LIVING THIS NAME

Christ, the Alpha and Omega, is Lord over the very beginnings and endings of our lives. Today is His, completely. All that concerns us from being born to dying is in His control. For example, Christ is master over the beginning and ending of my work, including all that concerns me about finding, holding, or even losing a job.

Christ likewise, the "author and finisher of our faith" (Heb. 12:2), is the initiator of life's every detail. He originates and creates all we need to start our journey as well as finish it. He not only authors, He finishes. Note how the Scriptures frequently remind us of this reality:

> He who has begun [alpha] a good work in you will complete it until [omega] the day of Jesus Christ (Phil. 1:6, brackets added).
>
> I know whom I have believed [alpha] and am persuaded that He is able to keep what I have committed to Him [omega] until that Day (2 Tim. 1:12, brackets added).

PRAYING THIS NAME

To pray in Jesus' name, our Alpha and Omega, is to saturate our prayers with the recognition that Christ alone is the totality of all we need. Getting answers to our prayers takes second place to meeting Jesus through prayer. He is the beginning and ending of all we could possibly desire. He is the ultimate answer to all our prayers.

Praying in Jesus' name, Alpha and Omega, means we infuse His fullness into every aspect of our day. We recognize that nothing escapes the sweep of His name. The "all and all" is with us. And because He controls all the power of eternity through His name, we need not fear any temporal difficulty. Christ not only was with each of us in all our yesterdays, He has gone before us into all our tomorrows.

Think of it! Tomorrow has yet to arrive, but Jesus is already there. He is our Alpha and Omega, and in Him we have the sum total of God's goodness. We can pray with Julian of Norwich:

> God, of Your goodness give me Yourself;
> For You are sufficient for me.
> I cannot properly ask anything less,
> to be worthy of You.
> If I were to ask less,
> I should always be in want.
> In You alone do I have all.[3]

TODAY'S PRAYER

I come to You, Lord,
as a creature caught within time.
So many of my days are too short;
so many of my trials seem too long;
so much of life seems scheduled by a clock
I want to control but can't.

I confess my sins of impatience and haste.
I have pressed issues before their time
and made shreds of what would have been blossoms.
I have hurried into situations
and created waves of confusion instead of bringing
Kingdom tranquility.

I need You, Lord.
You who transcend time—
you who are both the eternal Before
and the infinite Afterward—
come and fill my now.

Jesus, Alpha and Omega,
start writing what should be written in the whole
of my present circumstances.
You are able to author the story the Father intends,
and that's what I want.
I don't want to write with my own wisdom.
I've seen the end of those stories before,
and I don't like them.

So I pray today,
help me to live in Your name—
Jesus, Alpha and Omega.
You who know all that has preceded this moment
and what should flow out of it,
guide my path today—
in Your wisdom and for Your purposes.
Thank You, Lord,
In Jesus' name.
Amen.

HALLOWING THIS NAME

All and in All—Col. 3:11
Ancient of Days—Dan. 7:13-14
Beginning—Col. 1:18
Beginning of the Creation of God—Rev. 3:14
Blessed and Only Potentate—1 Tim. 6:15
Eternal Life—1 John 1:2
Everlasting Father—Isa. 9:6
First and the Last—Rev. 1:17
Forerunner—Heb. 6:20
God of the Whole Earth—Isa. 54:5
God the Judge of All—Heb. 12:23
He Who Fills All in All—Eph. 1:23
Heir of All Things—Heb. 1:2
I Am—John 8:58
Jehovah-Eloheka (The Lord Your God)—Ex. 20:2
Lord of All—Acts 10:36
Lord of All the Earth—Zech. 6:5
Lord over All—Rom. 10:12
Priest Forever—Heb. 5:6
Upholder of All Things—Heb. 1:3

17
THE LORD WHO HEALS
Exodus 15:26

RESTORATION

An attorney in a small midwestern town sent out letters notifying certain individuals that they had been named as benefactors in the will of a recently deceased elderly lady. One such individual, the woman's doctor of nearly four decades, was both surprised and curious. At the reading of the will the doctor was further startled to discover his ninety-year-old patient had left him a rather large trunk, tightly padlocked and hidden away for years in her attic. Some suspected the chest contained the woman's wealth.

Upon opening the trunk, however, all present were amazed to discover forty years worth of neatly packaged medical prescriptions, still in their bags, just as they had arrived from the local pharmacy. None had been opened; not a pill had been taken. It was the woman's way of saying, "Thanks, Doctor, for your concerns for my health, but I'll just trust the Lord who made my body to heal it."

KNOWING THIS NAME

Good health truly is one of life's priceless blessings. And God certainly has endowed the human body with an unusual capacity to heal itself (provided, of course, that it is cared for properly).

Even centuries before modern doctors spoke of "preventative medicine," God told Israel He wanted to spare them the numerous diseases plaguing Egypt (see Exod. 15:22-27). Just three days prior to issuing this promise, God had brought Israel miraculously through the Red Sea. Now they were traveling in a sweltering desert and found themselves without water. When they finally stumbled upon a pool of water at Marah, they quickly discovered it was unfit to drink, and Moses cried out to God in desperation.

The Lord responded by telling Moses to find a branch and toss it into the water. The patriarch obeyed and the waters instantly were purified or "healed." Immediately God told Moses, "If you listen carefully to the voice of the Lord your God and do what is right in His eyes, if you pay attention to His commands and keep all His decrees, I will not bring on you any of the diseases I brought on the Egyptians, for I am the Lord who heals you" (Exod. 15:26, NIV).

The expression "the Lord who heals" (Exod. 15:26) is derived from the Hebrew word *Jehovah-Rapha,* meaning literally "the Lord Healer." In Jeremiah 8:22 this same Hebrew word is translated "physician." This suggests the expression implies all that a physician might be and do, from caring for an illness throughout its duration to instructing a person in areas of wise health maintenance. Not only does the Lord promise to heal Israel (Exod. 15:26), but He specifically declares that His presence will prevent illness. He is saying, "I will not only heal you if you become ill, but I will keep the illness from you in the first place."

Thus, healing not only refers to recovery but to prevention or maintenance. In many cultures a physician is summoned not simply because a crisis occurs and immediate healing is required, but because a person desires advice and counsel concerning continued health. Even in our culture a high percentage of visits to the doctor involve physical exams rather than treatment for infirmities.

So it is with Jesus, who not only heals but sustains, and who not only delivers us from disease but directs us into health. It was Christ's style as God's incarnate Jehovah-Rapha to heal all who were sick (Matt. 12:15). And since Jesus has not changed (Heb. 13:8), we are given grounds for believing He cares about *our* sicknesses as well.

LIVING THIS NAME

Living in Jesus' name, the Lord Who Heals, begins with taking care of the temple in which God lives, our physical body (1 Cor. 6:19-20). If neglect of wise behavior, our unforgivingness or bitterness, or even outright abuse have brought us to the bed of affliction, the first thing we need to do is to confess these sins (1 John 1:9). But that's only the beginning. Christ promises health for body, soul, and spirit. He not only heals broken hearts (Ps. 147:3), He restores bruised souls (Luke 4:18, KJV) and heals us from our backslidings (Jer. 3:22). In short, Christ responds at every level of physical, emotional, mental, spiritual, and personal affliction. As the Psalmist said in summation, "He forgives all my sins and heals all my diseases (Ps. 103:3, NIV).

The context of this particular revelation of God's character as a healer (Exod. 15:22-27) is of particular significance to those who wish to live daily in this name of Jesus.

The bitter waters of Marah reflect the disappointments of life that can embitter the soul and sour our existence. (The use of water becomes an apt symbol since humans are comprised of over 90 percent water—and water is easily polluted or tainted.) Consider Israel's feeling of disappointment. At a distance they saw what appeared to be their salvation, a pool of refreshing water. It had been three days since anyone had had something to drink and serious dehydration was no doubt setting in. One can only imagine their feelings of utter despair when they discovered the water was unfit.

It was at this point in the narrative that Jesus' name took effect. God told Moses to find a branch (a prophetic picture of the coming Messiah as the prophet Jeremiah later would make clear in Jer. 23:5) and toss it into the water. And just as Moses' branch ultimately healed the bitter waters of Marah, Isaiah's subsequent prophecy (Isaiah 53) predicted the Messiah's suffering on the cross and the healing that would result from His action.

PRAYING THIS NAME

To pray today in Jesus' name, the Lord Who Heals, is to pray Jeremiah's prayer with confidence: "Heal me, O Lord, and I shall be healed." It is to recognize that Satan as the "prince of death" would seek to rob us of all that speaks of health. Therefore, he must be resisted in the power of Jesus' name, the Lord Who Heals.

Armed with God's Word and its multiplied promises for victorious, healthy living, we need to apply James' injunction: "Resist the devil and he will flee from you" (James 4:7).

Interestingly, the Greek word translated "resist" in James 4:7 (*histemi*) is the basis of the word translated "stand against" (*anthistemi*) in Ephesians 6:11, where Paul issues a challenge to "stand against the wiles of the devil." *Wiles* comes from the Greek word *methodias,* from which we derive our English word *method.* Again the message is clear. In prayer today we need to stand against all of Satan's methods which are designed to harass or hinder our health and happiness.

One specific thing to pray for is learning practical ways to fulfill God's requirements for health as found in our text for today's lesson, Exodus 15:26: "If you listen carefully to the voice of the Lord your God and do what is right in His eyes, if you pay attention to His commands and keep all His decrees, I will not bring on you any of the diseases I brought on the Egyptians, for I am the Lord who heals you" (NIV).

TODAY'S PRAYER

I call upon Your name, O Lord,
because in disclosing Yourself
as the Lord Who Heals
you have expressed Your nature.

Thank You for sending Jesus
to further remind us—
to remind me—
how great is Your love and
how unlimited is Your power to heal.
Now I come to ask that You hear my cry, for I am sick, Lord.
I am sick in body;
I am weary in soul;
I am tired in spirit;
I am in pain and torn with affliction.

I speak Your name, Jesus.
O Jesus, touch my body with health.

Lord Jesus, restore my soul and revive my spirit.
Healing Savior, remove my pain and repair my brokenness.
I cast all this burden upon Your back,
for it is there You bore the stripes
that purchased the healing
for which I now cry out.

I take Your name to my lips, my Healer—
and now, with praise to You,
I relax in Your promises and power
knowing all shall be well.
You are my Healing-Lord.
In Your name.
Amen.

HALLOWING THIS NAME

Balm in Gilead—Jer. 8:22
Fountain of Living Waters—Jer. 17:13-14
God of All Comfort—2 Cor. 1:3
Health of My Countenance—Ps. 42:11 (KJV)
Jehovah-Ropheka (The Lord Your Healer)—Exod. 15:26
Life-Giving Spirit—1 Cor. 15:45 (NIV)
My Strength—2 Sam. 22:33
Ointment Poured Forth—Song of Sol. 1:3
Physician—Luke 4:23
Prince of Life—Acts 3:15
Resting Place—Jer. 50:6
Restorer—Ps. 23:3
Resurrection and the Life—John 11:25
Strength of My Life—Ps. 27:1
Strength to the Needy—Isa. 25:4

18
THE BRIDEGROOM
Matthew 25:10

AFFECTION

"In the very beginning," observed Charles Spurgeon in his *Sermons*, "when this great universe lay in the mind of God, like unborn forests in the acorn cup; long before the echoes waked the solitudes, before the mountains were brought forth, and long before the light flashed through the sky, God loved its chosen creatures."[1]

Gerhard Tersteegen in *On Inward Prayer* adds, "This spirit of ours does not belong to this world, nor to temporal objects; it was created for God alone and therefore is capable of enjoying true fellowship with Him. It may be, and it ought to be, His temple and sacred residence. Its occupation is to contemplate, love, and enjoy this beneficent Being, and to repose in Him; for this end it was created."[2]

KNOWING THIS NAME

Affection is at the heart of the character of God, and at the heart of God's affection is the word *redemption*. Redemption, Christ's act of purchasing our salvation on the Cross, is an outflow of God's infinite love and affection for man. This was revealed in His desire to find a Bride for His Son, Jesus Christ. It is in this context that we look to Jesus, the Bridegroom (Matt. 25:10).

Christ's title, the Bridegroom, appears in one of our Lord's parables where He instructs His followers to be prepared for His return. In likening the Church to a bride awaiting the sudden, surprise appearance of her expected groom, Christ gives a tender portrayal of one aspect of His relationship with us. This isolated parable could be treated as merely a message of preparedness rather than one of relationship. However, other Scriptures speak of Christ's Church as His "bride," including three references in John's Revelation (Rev. 21:2, 9; 22:17). Paul likewise shows the parallel between a husband and wife and Christ and His Church (Eph. 5:22-33). It is from this latter passage that we learn most about the affection Jesus demonstrates toward His redeemed.

First, *Christ is the Savior who gave Himself for our redemption* (Eph. 5:23, 25). In laying down His life, our Lord has indicated not only the cost He was willing to pay for our salvation but the worth that He places upon us. We so often focus on the fact of our sin requiring the payment of death that we overlook an essential truth: Christ's love for us was so great that the cost was worth it to Him.

Second, *Christ is our Sanctifier who is patiently working with us to separate us completely unto Himself—and win us fully to Him* (Eph. 5:26). He does this, according to our text, by the cleansing power of the Word. How does this work? Ephesians 5:26 suggests that the washing of water by the Word is something Christ does as our heavenly Bridegroom. Here's a picture of Christ patiently and tenderly taking all of His promises and using them to cleanse our wounds, heal our bruises, and remove our stains. Like a loving bridegroom speaking comforting words to a hurt or troubled bride, Jesus takes time to administer His cleansing. He does this by releasing God's Word into our needs. He is not a harsh tyrant demanding perfection, rather He is a tender Redeemer loving us into wholeness and purity.

Third, *Christ is our Nourisher who holds us close to feed and strengthen us.* Interestingly, the words *nourish* and *cherish* in this text (Eph. 5:29) are words used to depict a nurse with a child. How powerfully this illustrates the affectionate way in which Christ has committed Himself to protect us, to answer each distressing call, to delight in drawing us near to feed and strengthen us. This terminology helps us grasp the picture of the Bridegroom whom Isaiah in another generation called "my Well-beloved" (Isa. 5:1).

LIVING THIS NAME

In his *Essays and Soliloquies*, Miguel de Unamuno wrote, "The living God, the human God, is reached not by way of reason but by way of love and suffering. It is not possible to know Him in order that afterwards we may later love Him; we must begin by loving Him, longing for Him, hungering for Him, before we can truly know Him."[3]

To live today in Jesus' name, our Bridegroom, is to renew our romance for Christ. And just as romance in a marriage is renewed by spending concentrated time with one's mate, so must we take time to fellowship lovingly with our Lord. Romance demands attention, and attention cultivates affection.

In considering Christ as the Bridegroom we especially should remember that this title is used when referring to His return for His Bride. All His affection for us culminates in His desire to "Come again and receive you to Myself; that where I am, there you may be also" (John 14:3). The appropriate response to His affection is that we cultivate affection for Him. And our eager anticipation of His coming should prompt us to purity of life, just as a bride keeps herself pure for her husband-to-be. John said, "We know that when He appears, we shall be like Him. . . . Everyone who has this hope in Him purifies himself, just as He is pure" (1 John 3:2-3, NIV). Alfred Lord Tennyson described this anticipation:

> He lifts me to the golden doors,
> The flashes come and go;
> All heaven bursts her starry floors,
> And strews her light below,
> And deepens on and up! The gates
> Roll back, and far within
> For me the Heavenly Bridegroom waits,
> To make me pure of sin. The Sabbaths of Eternity!
> One Sabbath deep and wide—
> a light upon the shining sea—
> the Bridegroom and the Bride.[4]

PRAYING THIS NAME

As we pray today in Jesus' name, our Bridegroom, time should be set aside just to love Him. Petitions sometimes clutter prayer.

Requests are fine, but they can wait until after worship. There'll be plenty of time for petitioning and interceding later. For now we'll just reach out and hold the hands of Jesus. Like the bride on her wedding night who longs only to be held by her bridegroom and lover, so may we desire only to be held tightly in the arms of Christ. Worship Him. Exalt Him. Yearn for Him. Hunger after Christ alone.

Thomas More, the sixteenth-century scholar who died for his religious convictions, learned to cultivate this desire for Christ. It was More's brilliant gifts that opened the doors for him to various positions with the government of King Henry VIII. One such post was Chancellor of the Exchequer, a position equivalent to that in the high cabinet in America's government today. However, when Henry VIII decided to obtain a divorce, Thomas More, convinced such action violated God's Law, opposed him. He told the King, "I am the King's good servant, but God is first!" This remark, history records, resulted in the scholar's execution.

But even on the scaffold More demonstrated his confidence in Christ, his lover and companion. Condemned but still rejoicing, More told his executioner, "Assist me up. Coming down, I can shift for myself." Equally memorable is More's prayer offered earlier in his life:

> Give me, good Lord, a longing to be
> With You, not to avoid the calamities
> Of this world, nor so much to attain
> The joys of heaven, as simply for love
> Of You.
> And give me, good Lord, Your love and
> Favor, which my love of You, however
> Great it might be, could not deserve
> Were it not for Your great goodness.
> These things, good Lord, that I pray
> For, give me Your grace to labor for.[5]

TODAY'S PRAYER

Dear God,
Like Isaiah, who long ago said,
"I live amid a people of unclean lips and am that way myself,"
I come before You today.

There is so much pollution in my world, Father,
it seems that purity is a lost art for living.
But I come to be embraced by a love
so pure and powerful,
so comforting and keeping,
that the world-spirit has never been able to reduce its worth
or pollute its preciousness.

In the name of Jesus,
the heavenly Bridegroom,
I come today to be caught up in the arms of
eternal love and purifying fire.
By Your faithfulness, Jesus, keep me faithful.
By Your holiness, Savior, make me holy.
By Your loving-kindness, Lord, make the love I extend to others
bridegroom-like: both loving and kind.

I anticipate the day of Your coming again, Lord Jesus.
But until that day,
and amid these last days so infected with sin and sinning,
I choose to live in the provisions of Your name.
Today, in the name of the Bridegroom,
I live with hope and holiness.
By Your great love and power.
And in Your name.
Amen.

HALLOWING THIS NAME

Altogether Lovely—Song of Sol. 5:16
Bundle of Myrrh—Song of Sol. 1:13
Cluster of Henna Blossoms—Song of Sol. 1:14
God Full of Compassion—Ps. 86:15
God of Comfort—Rom. 15:5
God of Love and Peace—2 Cor. 13:11
Head of the Body—Col. 1:18
Lily of the Valleys—Song of Sol. 2:1
Love—1 John 4:16
My Beloved—Matt. 12:1; Song of Sol. 2:16
My Song—Isa. 12:2
My Well-beloved—Isa. 5:1
One My Heart Loves—Song of Sol. 3:2 (NIV)
Rose of Sharon—Song of Sol. 2:1

19
WONDERFUL
COUNSELOR
Isaiah 9:6

INSIGHT

Henry Martyn, a brilliant British linguist who died in 1812 at the youthful age of thirty-one, had an unusual distinction. He was the first Englishman to offer himself as a candidate for the newly-formed Church Missionary Society in England as well as the first to be rejected by the same society. Yet, unwilling to be denied his calling, Martyn went to India as a chaplain for the East India Company.

There Martyn translated the New Testament into Hindustani and later went to Persia, where he translated it into Arabic and Persian. During times of deep frustration with these languages, Henry Martyn learned to cry out in Jesus' name for anointed insight to accomplish his difficult task. With simplicity and candor Martyn prayed:

> Lord, I am blind and helpless,
> Stupid and ignorant.
> Cause me to hear;
> Cause me to know;
> Teach me to do;
> Lead me.[1]

Through it all, Martyn mastered an understanding of biblical patterns of prayer. He recognized that a considerable number of the prayers of the Bible were not requests for material blessings but for spiritual insight. The psalmist, for example, repeatedly offered such petitions as "Show me," "Lead me," "Teach me," "Direct me," "Instruct me," and "Guide me." Paul likewise emphasized this reality in his personal prayers. To the Colossians he wrote, "Since the day we heard about you, we have not stopped praying for you and asking God to fill you with the knowledge of His will through all spiritual wisdom and understanding" (Col. 1:9, NIV).

To the Philippians Paul said, "And this is my prayer: that your love may abound more and more in knowledge and depth of insight, so that you may be able to discern what is best . . . " (Phil. 1:9-10, NIV).

Both the Apostle Paul and Henry Martyn had learned a vital secret: praying in Jesus' name means receiving counsel and insight at their highest levels, for Jesus Christ is our Wonderful Counselor!

KNOWING THIS NAME

It is Isaiah who introduces us to one of the most familiar prophetic designations given the Messiah: Wonderful Counselor (Isa. 9:6). Isaiah is here foretelling of One who will come as the ultimate answer to Israel's every problem. This prophecy came during a time of great disturbance in Judah. There was a need for a king who would not only rule in power, but who would be able to bring "wise counsel" into troubling situations and help resolve them.

Most of us can identify with these feelings of frustration. Periodically we all find ourselves faced with problems that defy solutions. But in Jesus' name, our Wonderful Counselor, we can find help.

In evaluating our text, Isaiah 9:6, Hebrew scholar Franz Delitzsch makes several meaningful observations concerning Christ, our Wonderful Counselor:

> The name of Jesus is the combination of all the Old Testament titles used to designate the Coming One according to His nature and His works. The names contained in Isaiah 7:14 and 9:6 are not thereby suppressed; but they have continued, from the time of Mary downwards, in the

mouths of all believers. There is not one of these names under which worship and homage have not been paid to him. But we never find them crowded together anywhere else as we do here in Isaiah; and in this respect also our prophet proves himself the greatest of the Old Testament evangelists.[2]

Delitzsch also notes how the seventy translators of the Septuagint (the Greek translation of the Old Testament from the Hebrew) joined the two words Wonderful Counselor in their translation, literally describing Christ as the "One counseling wonderful things." An alternative translation renders it "a wonder of a counselor."

The thought is that in Christ a union occurs between His wonder-working essence (that is, a person filled with wonders, a person "wonderful" in his own right) and a counselor of heavenly origin who brings divine insight into human difficulties.

The first occurrence of the singular title Wonderful is found in Judges 13:17-18. The original King James Version translates the phrase, "Why askest thou thus after my name, seeing it is secret?" But the literal translation of the word *secret* used in the King James Version is "wonderful." It directly relates to the next verse (v. 19) which says of the angel with whom Manoah spoke, "And the angel did wonderously; and Manoah and his wife looked on." The birth of Samson on the heels of this "wonderful" angelic visitation is yet another example of God visiting His people with wonderful answers for worrisome situations.

The Hebrew words translated *secret* (KJV) and *wonderful* (NKJV) are taken from the Hebrew word *pehleh* meaning "a marvel, a miracle, or a wonderful thing." The NIV translates it as "beyond understanding" (Judg. 13:18) and "an amazing thing" (Judg. 13:19). Interestingly, *pehleh's* primary root *pawlaw,* which means "great, marvelous, or wonderful," has a fundamental meaning of "to separate or distinguish." Obviously the idea of these words is that this title of the coming Messiah, Wonderful, is indicative of the fact that He stands out far over and above and separate from every other source of ability or counsel. There is none comparable!

And when this expression *Wonderful* is combined with the term *Counselor* (from the Hebrew word *yawats* meaning "to advise, resolve, or guide"), we have an exciting concept of One who gives

114

amazing advice "beyond understanding"; One whose advice is a wonder!

LIVING THIS NAME

Living in Jesus' name, our Wonderful Counselor, is to face today's activities anticipating an inexhaustible supply of His wonderful insight—insight that flows from a supernatural vantage point. Because Christ sees all there is to see, His counsel, instruction, teaching, and direction are all we need to navigate the labyrinth of today's every circumstance. Further, our confidence increases as we realize Jesus not only *gives* insight, He *is* Insight—the literal personification of divine understanding.

When someone receives Christ as his Savior, he is usually told that Jesus has come into his heart to dwell personally within him. The Apostle John tells us this is true (John 14:23). And since Christ, who is the personification of divine insight, can be expected to speak from where He lives (the hearts of believers), we must learn to listen "within" for His advice and counsel. If what we hear in our hearts is really of God, we can rest assured that His Word (Heb. 4:12) along with the wise counsel of Spirit-led advisers (Prov. 20:18; 15:22) will confirm it.

PRAYING THIS NAME

The hymn writer Charles C. Converse wrote, "O what peace we often forfeit, O what needless pain we bear, all because we do not carry everything to God in prayer!"

Insight for today is but a prayer away if we'll just learn to listen. Too many of us are like Joshua who, after seeking "insight" from his Captain prior to his triumph at Jericho (Josh. 5:13-15), failed to seek similar counsel before what became his defeat at Ai (Josh. 7:2-5). Think of the "needless pain" Joshua had to deal with as Achan's sin was discovered and the peace Israel had to forfeit for a time.

But before we move into the day trusting Christ to be our Wonderful Counselor, we need to spend some quality time with Him alone. We need to let Him show us the day through His eyes. After all, Jesus didn't just say "pray." He said, "Watch and pray" (Matt. 26:41). He was saying, "Be alert to the subtleties of Satan and the potential failures of the flesh that might await you this day."

Beloved, Satan would seek to seduce us today and "sift us as wheat," seeking to defeat us as he sought Peter's defeat (Luke 22:31). We must prayerfully anticipate these occasions and in Jesus' name, our Wonderful Counselor, seek insight to avoid them. Whom will we meet? Where will we go? What are our plans? Is temptation waiting in some future hidden moment? Christ will warn us if we'll stay close to Him. He, after all, is our insight—and insight is "the power or act of seeing into a situation." So, while we are "looking unto Jesus" (Heb. 12:2), He will be looking out for us (John 10:28).

TODAY'S PRAYER

Someone has said, Lord—
sometime,
somewhere—
someone said,
"It's a jungle out there."

He was talking about this world You created
in beauty and perfection,
but which has degenerated so sadly because
of our having dragged it all down with us
when we fell—we humankind.

Dear Lord, this jungle is my address.
I'm not blaming You for the animal-like behavior of
people who prey on each other.
Nor am I complaining about the confusing overgrowth of
situations which prevent a clear view ahead.
I simply come to state my situation and make my prayer.

I'm so thankful for You, Jesus,
my Wonderful Counselor,
who is present every step I take to give
insight,
wisdom,
perspective,
and knowledge beyond my own.

Today, as I step over the threshold
into the demands of daily duty,
I vow to make this commitment:
I proceed in Your name,
depending upon Your moment-by-moment assistance
helping me to know what to do and how to do it.
I expect to penetrate the jungle
with something of heaven's life and beauty today.
In Jesus' name.
Amen.

HALLOWING THIS NAME

Chief Shepherd—1 Pet. 5:4
Faithful and True Witness—Rev. 3:14
Friend Who Sticks Closer than a Brother—Prov. 18:24
Good Shepherd—John 10:11
Good Teacher—Mark 10:17
Great Light—Isa. 9:2
Habitation of Justice—Jer. 50:7
Judge and Lawgiver—Isa. 33:22
Lord God of Israel—Exod. 34:23
My Shepherd (Jehovah-Rohi)—Ps. 23:1
One Shepherd—John 10:16
Only Wise God—1 Tim. 1:17
Rabbi—John 1:49
Spirit of Justice—Isa. 28:5-6
Understanding—Prov. 8:14
Wisdom—Prov. 8:12
Wisdom of God—1 Cor. 1:24
Word of Life—1 John 1:1

20
THE HEADSTONE
OF THE CORNER
Psalm 118:22

COMPLETION

God has a plan of ultimate completion for His universe, and Christ clearly is the focus of that plan. Phillips Brooks, best known for his Christmas carol "O Little Town of Bethlehem," put this in perspective: "Slowly, through all the universe the temple of God is being built. And whenever, in any place, a soul by free-willed obedience, catches the fire of God's likeness, it is set into the growing walls, a living stone."[1] Dante, in *The Divine Comedy*, adds, "I raised my eyes aloft, and I beheld the scattered chapters of the universe gathered and bound into a single book by the austere and tender hand of God."[2]

KNOWING THIS NAME

That Christ is the "centerpiece" of God's eternal plan is emphasized by the psalmist's use of the phrase "Headstone of the Corner" or "Chief Cornerstone" in reference to our Lord (Ps. 118:22). The literal biblical meaning of Headstone of the Corner or Chief Cornerstone as rendered by the NKJV is only fully understood when we note that the practice of placing the cornerstone in ancient Israel differs from how we generally place it today. Then, as today, this stone was the last to be put in place. Usually this placement was accompanied by ceremonies indicating a building's completion. Today we place the stone at or near ground level. In ancient Israel, however, it was placed at the very top—a true "head" stone. For that reason, the chief stone (i.e., headstone) stood high above all else. Sometimes it even was made of a different material than the other stones as a silent reminder of its superior role and place in proclaiming a project's completion.

It is because the material of the headstone might, on occasion, be slightly different that we understand the words: "The stone which the builders rejected has become the chief cornerstone" (Ps. 118:22). Christ, the stone, was rejected because He was different. He didn't fit their preconceptions or specifications.

Other translations describe the Headstone of the Corner as: "the main Cornerstone" (NEB); "the Key Stone" (The Jerusalem Bible); "the Capstone" (NIV); "the most important Stone" (TEV); and, "the honored Cornerstone" (TLB). In every case, the concept relates to the "Stone of Completion."

The significance of this title of Christ is twofold. First, it demonstrates the fact that He completes God's working in our lives, and second, it signifies the way He surprises us with His methods. Our human reasoning too often would preempt the possibilities God has in mind for us. Prayer in Jesus' name, the Headstone of the Corner, can serve to cement in us this twofold reminder: We can be certain Christ will finish what He is doing in or for us, and we can take comfort in knowing we don't need to be able to figure out how He eventually will get the job done. He may even wish to surprise us!

Other references to this aspect of Christ's person as the Headstone of the Corner are found throughout the New Testament (Matt. 21:42; Mark 12:10; Luke 20:17). Significantly, it was this very title of Christ that Peter and John referred to (Acts 4:11) when they were forbidden by religious leaders to teach or speak in Jesus' name. If anyone questioned whether they were referring to Christ, the question was answered in Peter's very next breath: "Nor is there salvation in any other, for there is no other name under heaven given among men by which we must be saved" (Acts 4:12).

LIVING THIS NAME

Reminding believers that they were citizens of another land, Paul wrote: "Now therefore, you are no longer strangers and foreigners, but fellow citizens with the saints and members of the household of God, having been built on the foundation of the apostles and prophets, Jesus Christ Himself being the chief cornerstone" (Eph. 2:19-20).

Here the apostle was picturing Christ as the central, focal, foundational point of reference in the building (and completion) of the Church (see also Matt. 16:18). And since we are a part of Christ's Church, living today in Jesus' name, the Headstone of the Corner, is to live in His power to complete all that He has begun within each of us.

Christ, after all, sacrificed His very life to "complete" our salvation. His scars bear the mark of our completion. It's not without significance that we often inscribe statements on cornerstones in the process of dedicating the buildings in which they are placed. We might note that Christ's body, too, was "engraved," but with scars indicating His dedication to our complete forgiveness, redemption, healing, and salvation—today!

Further, memorabilia and messages often are placed within a cornerstone in the hopes that future generations will discover them and remember the past. Similarly, all the fullness of God has been hidden in Christ, the Headstone of the Corner, including God's infinite riches and immutable promises. As we live today in Jesus' name we rest in the fullness of His completion, for Paul said plainly, "You are complete in Him!" (Col. 2:10). So whether approaching the task of doing housework, working on a job, or even engaging in leisure activity, we are complete in Christ, the Headstone of the Corner. His presence towers above each day declaring, "He who calls you is faithful, who also will do it" (1 Thess. 5:24).

PRAYING THIS NAME

To pray in Jesus' name, the Headstone of the Corner, is to search out areas of the day in which we might project Christ's miracle capacity to "complete" what remains unfinished in our lives.

Do you have any loose ends lingering amid the clutter of incomplete intentions? Is there something missing in your maturing process or an unresolved resentment restraining a relationship? Today in Jesus' name, the Headstone of the Corner, you can claim Christ's power to work completion in every area of your life where neglect has limited growth—especially areas of total surrender and self-control.

Enabled by Christ, the Chief Cornerstone, we can cry out with Desiderius Erasmus, the fifteenth-century saint:

> Sever me from myself that I may
> Be grateful to You;
> May I perish to myself that I
> May be safe in You;
> May I die to myself that I
> May live in You;
> May I wither to myself that
> I may blossom in You;
> May I be emptied of myself that
> I may abound in You;
> May I be nothing to myself that
> I may be all to You.[3]

TODAY'S PRAYER

Hear my prayer, Dear Father.
I offer it in the name of Jesus,
the Headstone of the Corner.

I bow to offer You all the plans I have for today . . .
or, for that matter, for all of my life.
I want You to keep any blueprints I draw
under the control of Your design and wisdom,
for I know I am all too capable of
trying to build things that won't last.

I ask You, Lord,
please demolish anything in my life
that isn't according to Your specifications
or that doesn't merit Your crowning seal of approval.
Help me hear Your voice
and do Your will.

This day with this prayer
I ask that this name dominate all that concerns me:
Jesus—the Cornerstone.

I want to build upon You, knowing that
Your surprises are better than my carefully laid plans.

Help me, O Lord God.
I don't want any sand
under the footings of
my life's foundations.
In Jesus' name.
Amen.

HALLOWING HIS NAME

Banner to the People—Isa. 11:10
Chief Cornerstone—1 Pet. 2:6
Elect Stone—1 Pet. 2:6
Finisher of Our Faith—Heb. 12:2
Jesus Christ the Righteous—1 John 2:1
Living Stone—1 Pet. 2:4
Precious Stone—1 Pet. 2:6
Stone—Matt. 21:42
Stone of Israel—Gen. 49:24
Stone of Stumbling—1 Pet. 2:8
Tried Stone—Isa. 28:16

21
THE LIFTER UP
OF MY HEAD
Psalm 3:3

CONFIDENCE

Trained counselors are quick to caution clients that if they truly desire victory over problems they must first remove "I can't" from their vocabularies. "I can't get along with my wife"; "I can't quit smoking"; "I can't control my temper"; "I can't hold down a job"; "I can't witness for Jesus." The list is as long as those tasks we deem difficult, and no doubt each of us has been plagued by the "I can't" syndrome at one time or another.

In just ten words, however, Paul destroys the "I can't" myth in a single, all-encompassing confession: "I can do all things through Christ who strengthens me" (Phil. 4:13). Expanding Paul's words, *The Amplified Bible* reads: "I have strength for all things in Christ Who empowers me—I am ready for anything and equal to anything through Him Who infuses inner strength into me. In other words, I am self-sufficient in Christ's sufficiency."

When Paul says we can do anything "through Christ," he is reminding us that our confidence and power is in Christ who lifts us above circumstances that might otherwise defeat us. The psalmist said it simply: "But You, O Lord, are . . . the One who lifts up my head" (Ps. 3:3).

KNOWING THIS NAME

It is in fleeing from his son Absalom that David introduces us to our Lord as the "Lifter Up of My Head." It is in this circumstance in Psalm 3 that Israel's shepherd-king pictures the Lord as a "shield," "my glory," and the "lifter up of my head" (KJV). The whole of this psalm outlines the meaning of this phrase "the lifter up of my head." It is a psalm that moves from a desperate cry in the midst of trouble to a concluding declaration of confidence in the Lord's power to deliver. The psalm begins, "Lord, how they have increased who trouble me! Many are they who rise up against me. Many are they who say of me, 'There is no help for him in God'" (vv. 1-2), and ends with this confident assessment: "Salvation belongs to the Lord. Your blessing is upon Your people" (v. 8). This turnaround of the soul from confusion to confidence centers on the assertion, "You, Lord, are . . . the One who lifts up my head."

"Head" used in this verse relates to a person's rights, authority, or position. David is essentially saying, "What and who I am is being assaulted." In fact, Absalom was trying to steal David's kingdom. The introduction to this psalm in the Hebrew Psalter reads, "A psalm of David when he fled from Absalom his son." Such is the historical context of this title of Christ.

Four entire chapters in 2 Samuel report Absalom's treason against his father's rule. Noteworthy is David's refusal to assert his own authority. He was determined instead to allow the Lord to defend him. Consider, for example, David's words when Shimei, a representative of Saul's camp, curses David as he flees from Jerusalem in the wake of Absalom's takeover: "It may be that the Lord will look on my affliction, and that the Lord will repay me with good for his cursing this day" (2 Sam. 16:12).

The lesson of our text (Ps. 3:3) and its portrayal of Christ as the Lifter Up of My Head is that in Him we have One who will not forget us when opposition arises. He will come to our ultimate defense even though the present circumstance seems to indicate failure. David is saying, "Lord, You're the one who will lift up my fallen, rejected-by-man rights." This is not a passive, "wimpy" posture; no matter how it may appear to natural man. David actually is being assertive. Here is a psalm exalting the one who alone establishes authority, rights, and power. Here is a confession of faith that God alone is able to restore what man attacks or steals. The basis for our confidence is simply this: No one can take from any of us what God wants us to have. If it appears stolen or seized, our resort is the Lord—he is the one who "lifts up" (i.e., raises, elevates, exalts) our places, privileges, positions, or person.

LIVING THIS NAME

Living today in Jesus' name, the Lifter Up of My Head, is to move into the day trusting that we will be saturated with Christ's confidence. God knows our weaknesses as well as our strengths, and He can strengthen the weaknesses and maximize the strengths. It is His nature to "lift up."

When we apply this title of Christ, it is helpful to remember the Hebrew origin of the expression "lifts up" (Ps. 3:3). The expression comes from the Hebrew word *ruhm* and is used in a number of interesting ways throughout the Old Testament. It is used to describe the raising up or building of a house (Ezra 9:9); the causing of a plant to grow by watering it (Ezek. 31:4); the placing of someone in a safe place (Pss. 27:5; 18:49); and the raising up of children (Isa. 1:2; 23:4). How encouraging it is to consider the implication of the Lord's capacity to lift up those matters that concern our home, our work, our provision, our safety, and even the raising of our children. All of this results from learning to live in Jesus' name—the Lifter Up of My Head.

So we need not strive to raise ourselves up, for Christ will lift us up. By God's grace we can rid our vocabularies of every "I can't." In *Stones and Bread* Gerald Vann wrote, "Trying to be perfect means trying to do your particular best, with the particular graces God has given you. You cannot pray like Saint Teresa anymore than you can sing like Caruso, but how foolish if for that reason you give up trying to pray or sing at all. What God asks of you is that you should do your best, not Saint Teresa's best."[1]

Be quick, today, beloved, to recognize the personal attention our Lord is ready to give when our heads hang low because of circumstance, discouragement, or outright opposition. Just as surely as we are commanded to lift up the weary hands or feeble legs of those struggling in life's battles (Heb. 12:12-13), our Lord, the Lifter Up of My Head, is gracious to invade our day and lift us above our fears and failures.

PRAYING THIS NAME

In prayer today anticipate each circumstance that might require special confidence. Is there a difficult task to be faced in the hours just ahead? Have you recently encountered a spirit of depression that makes you feel as if you're walking in spiritual quicksand? Picture that difficult task or spirit of depression and visually imagine Christ coming to you and lifting your head gently with His tender touch. Can you feel Him raising you up even now? He not only lifts your head but in the process lifts you to your feet in confidence, just as He lifted Daniel after the prophet had fallen in fear before the presence of Christ (Dan. 10:1-12).

Beloved reader, don't give Satan even an inch today in allowing condemnation to limit your effectiveness in prayer. Nor can you let the enormity of your problems paint a picture of impossibility even before you approach God's throne to petition Him for power. There'll be many days you'll feel like praying with those Breton fisherman of France, "Dear God, be good to me. The sea is so wide, and my boat is so small."[2] But thankfully, the magnitude of those circumstances will melt in a moment when you realize that Christ, the Lifter Up of My Head, is sitting right beside you in the boat. With confidence you will be able to say with Tennyson the following words from *In Memorium:*

> And all is well, tho' faith and form
> Be sunder'd in the night of fear;
> Well roars the storm to those that hear
> A deeper voice across the storm.[3]

TODAY'S PRAYER

I am moved today, Lord,
in thinking how completely You have provided
for the restoration of everything that has fallen in man.

My head is often downcast, Lord,
because of factors that flow from that fall:
My head falls because I'm ashamed of my sin
or my cowardice or my foolishness;
my head falls because people assail me
or criticize or don't understand me;
my head falls because I lose confidence
or hope or faith that things will work out.

But today, hope rises.
I'm reminded that You not only love,
save,

forgive,
and redeem,
but You lean over to take me in Your arms.
You stretch forth Your hands
to take my crestfallen spirit and,
Lord, You lift up my head!
Like a father assuring a heartbroken son,
like a mother comforting a bruised and frightened child,
You lift up my head!

And I hear You speaking to me from Your Word,
"I am Your glory and the Lifter Up of Your head."
And my heart says, amen, Lord.
And thank You.
In Jesus' name.
Amen.

HALLOWING THIS NAME

Consolation of Israel—Luke 2:25
Deliverer—Rom. 11:26
God of Comfort—Rom. 15:5
God of Hope—Rom. 15:13
Hope of Israel—Jer. 14:8
Hope of Their Fathers—Jer. 50:7
Lamb of God—John 1:29
My Help—Ps. 115:11
My Hope—Ps. 71:5
My Shepherd—Ps. 23
My Strength and My Song—Isa. 12:2
One Who Will Have Dominion—Num. 24:19
Our Hope—1 Tim. 1:1
Strength to the Needy—Isa. 25:4

22

MY ROCK
Psalm 31:3

REFUGE

In his *Unspoken Sermons,* penned a century ago, George MacDonald advised, "That man is perfect in faith who can come to God in the utter dearth of his feelings and desires, without a glow of aspiration, with the weight of low thoughts, failures, neglects, and wandering forgetfulness, and say to Him, 'Thou art my refuge.' "[1]

King David surely fits MacDonald's measure of a man of faith, for few in Scripture suffered the setbacks of this anointed king. Perhaps this is why David provides us with so many glimpses of the Lord's nature and character as revealed in His many titles, including our title for today: My Rock (Ps. 31:3).

It was out of suffering that David could point to his Lord as a place of refuge. In the context of this title David says, "My life is spent . . . my strength fails . . . my bones waste away. . . . I am forgotten like a dead man . . . " (Ps. 31:10, 12). But David had learned that no matter what the trial, he could pray with assurance, "You are my rock and my fortress; therefore, for Your name's sake, lead me and guide me" (Ps. 31:3).

KNOWING THIS NAME

Throughout Scripture our Lord is frequently identified by the title "Rock." He is "the rock" upon which the church is built (Matt.

128

16:18; Eph. 2:20). He is our "rock of refuge" (Psa. 31:2). He is our "everlasting rock" (Isa. 26:4, *The Amplified Bible*), an expression translated "Rock eternal" in the New International Version. He is the "rock that is higher than I" (Ps. 61:2); "that spiritual Rock" (1 Cor. 10:4); "my rock" and "my fortress" (Ps. 31:3); and "the Rock of my salvation" (2 Sam. 22:47).

Each of these biblical revelations of our Lord features unique facets of our Rock. He shelters, He gives foundation, He provides a defense against the enemy, He nourishes and protects during trials and troubles, and He assures a secure footing as we step into each new day. But whatever the idea, the essential focus of the title "Rock" is that there is an exalted, elevated, out-of-reach location available to the person who would take refuge in Christ's name.

The Hebrew word in Psalm 31:3-4 for "rock" is *sehlah*. We gain an idea of the degree of protective refuge that is intended by using this Hebrew word when we discover that *Sela* (from *sehlah*) was the name of an ancient Edomite city. The descendants of Esau called this city "Rock" because it was a natural fortress of refuge. And the Greeks later named the same city "Petra," their word for rock.

There are few comparable locations to Petra on the face of the earth today. This city was virtually impregnable against attack by the military technology and weaponry of the ancient world. The primary access to this stronghold was, and continues to be, a very narrow, natural gorge called the *Sik* (Arabic for "shaft") which is about a mile in length and approximately ten feet wide. Because of this geological factor, the Sik could easily be defended by even a tiny band of people against any invasion, even when the attackers used suicide tactics. As G. A. Smith notes in his commentary, "The interior is reached by defiles (gorges) so narrow that two horsemen may scarcely ride abreast, and the sun is shut out by the overhanging rocks." What a powerful picture of our Lord, who is our Rock and Fortress—our hiding place and refuge from every storm.

LIVING THIS NAME

As unpleasant as the thought may be, it is possible that storm clouds are gathering on the horizons of the day. We would do well to prepare for this possibility so we can face each storm securely in Jesus' name, our Rock. Especially encouraging is the reality that we not only dwell in the Rock but the Rock dwells in us. The world has its slogan: "May the 'force' be with you." But we have the reality: The Fortress is within us! As Ralph Waldo Emerson wrote in *Self Reliance,* "Let us stun and astonish the intruding rabble of men and books and institutions by a simple declaration of the divine fact. Bid the invaders take the shoes from off their feet, for God is here within."[2]

Psalm 31:2-3 describes the Lord not only as our "rock" and "fortress" but as our "rock of refuge." The Hebrew words used here are *metsoodaw* (fortress) and *maoz* (refuge). They combine to describe the following: "A place of escape or defense conveying the idea of a city that, should the enemy seek to overthrow it, he himself will be overthrown." In this sense the words employed in this psalm carry the idea of a snare or a trap.

Think of it! The traps Satan places before us today will be turned by Christ into traps that will snare Satan himself.

Interestingly, in the same way that *sehlah* (rock) brings the city of Petra (Sela) to mind, so *metsoodaw* (fortress) brings the famous natural fortress Masada (derived from *metsoodaw)* into focus. Masada was a towering natural fortress used by Herod the Great as a military outpost just before the time of Christ. The fortress was built on a butte or mesa, which rises more than fourteen hundred feet above the level of the nearby Dead Sea. It was here in 70 to 73 A.D. that Jewish zealots sustained a revolt against the Roman Empire. And they resisted Rome three years longer than any other segment of their guerrilla forces simply because of the strength of their position in the Masada.

In a similar way, we too may sometimes feel weak and weaponless as we face our adversary. But we must never forget our position is in Christ, our *Sehlah Metsoodaw!*

PRAYING THIS NAME

To pray today in Jesus' name, our Rock, is to pray in the recognition that Christ is our refuge for every situation we might face. And because those storm clouds mentioned earlier often appear well before a storm, we should take time in prayer to scan the horizon of the day for telltale signs of difficulty. If we sense a storm is developing we can appropriate the power of Christ, our Rock, into that situation. Naturally, the darker the clouds the greater the possible severity of the storm. And the greater the possible severity of the storm, the farther into the Fortress we'll need to go. This suggests there will be times when we need to spend extra moments resting in our Rock.

Beloved, when Jesus taught us to pray "deliver us from the evil one" (Matt. 6:13), He was teaching us to assume a warfare stance in prayer—a stance that doesn't mean so much a rushing head-long into battle as a prompt retreating into our "Strong Tower," Christ Himself (see Prov. 18:10).

Seasoned warriors of prayer learn to fight their battles from the throne room of God where we "sit together" with Christ "in heavenly places" (Eph. 2:6). Our prayer closets, beloved, are the places where all spiritual battles really are won. S. D. Gordon wrote, "The real victory in all service is won beforehand in prayer. Service is merely gathering up the results."[3]

And because God inhabits or dwells in the praises of Israel, His people (Ps. 22:3), the best way to insure that God's presence "inhabits" our prayer closets is to fill them with praise. Once again, praise becomes a vital quality of praying effectively "in Jesus' name!"

TODAY'S PRAYER

Lord, today in praise with William B. Bradbury I declare:

> My hope is built on nothing less
> Than Jesus' blood and righteousness;
> I dare not trust the sweetest frame,
> But wholly lean on Jesus' name.
> When darkness veils His lovely face;
> I rest on His unchanging grace;
> In every high and stormy gale,
> My anchor holds within the veil.
> On Christ the solid rock, I stand;
> All other ground is sinking sand,
> All other ground is sinking sand.

HALLOWING THIS NAME
Cover—Isa. 32:2
Hiding Place from the Wind—Isa. 32:2

Hope of His People—Joel 3:16 (KJV)
Horn of Salvation—Luke 1:69
Lord, Mighty in Battle—Ps. 24:8
Lord, Strong and Mighty—Ps. 24:8
My Fortress—Ps. 18:2
My Rock of Refuge—Ps. 31:2
Refuge from the Storm—Isa. 25:4
Rock of Offense—1 Pet. 2:8; Isa. 8:14
Rock That Is Higher than I—Ps. 61:2
Sanctuary—Isa. 8:14
Shade from the Heat—Isa. 25:4
Shadow of a Great Rock in a Weary Land—Isa. 32:2
Stone Cut Out without Hands—Dan. 2:34-35
Strong Tower—Ps. 61:3
Stronghold—Nahum 1:7
That Spiritual Rock—1 Cor. 10:4
Tower of Salvation—2 Sam. 22:51

23
THE POWER OF GOD
1 Corinthians 1:24

MASTERY

Pete and his friends had been warned by their high school counselors not to stray from the picnic area at their senior class outing. In recent weeks a murder and several rapes had occurred on the far side of that particular lake. But even though Pete was a born-again Christian, he had that streak of curiosity most teenagers have, and just minutes after the buses arrived he and his friends slipped away from the group and headed for the far side of the lake.

Never believing it could happen to them, Pete and his friends were shocked when confronted by a group of Hells Angels as they passed through a remote wooded area. Suddenly one of the bikers, the ringleader, pulled a switchblade bigger than the teens had ever seen. According to Pete he was so afraid he couldn't speak.

"I tried to speak the name of Jesus, but I couldn't talk," Pete later told his church youth group. "All I could do was think of the verse, 'Greater is He that is in you, than he that is in the world' " (1 John 4:4, KJV).

Pete continued, "Don't ask me to explain this, but the minute I thought that verse, the big guy with the knife started shaking all over. He could hardly hold onto his switchblade. We couldn't believe it. He took about three steps backwards and said, 'You're just lucky I'm in a good mood today because we're going to let you go,' and he turned and motioned for the others to go. They practically ran into the bushes."

KNOWING THIS NAME

There's something supernatural about the name of Jesus, whether it is thought or spoken. His name is the personification of power, vitality, dynamics, and strength. In a word, Jesus' name means "mastery."

Paul introduces us to this idea when he ascribes to Christ the title "the Power of God" (1 Cor. 1:24). Here the apostle presents our Lord as the Power of God in two respects: first, as the result of Christ's work on the Cross, and second, in contrast to all human notions of power. The essence of the idea is that to pray in Jesus' name places us within the resources of Calvary's almightiness and beyond the resources of man's very best workings or reasonings.

A better understanding of the significance of this title is marvelously demonstrated in the wealth of words used in the Greek New Testament to describe Christ as the Power of God.

First, *Jesus is our miracle!* Note our text for today (1 Cor. 1:24), where Paul refers to Christ as the Power of God, along with the apostle's reference to Christ as "the Son of God *with power,* according to the Spirit of holiness, by the resurrection from the dead" (Rom. 1:4; italics added). The Greek word translated "power" in these two passages is *dunamis,* from which we get our word *dynamo.* The basic meaning is "extraordinary force" or "supernatural power." Because the word describes that which is "above the ordinary," it is also translated "miracle" in the New Testament. (See Mark 9:39; Acts 2:22; 1 Cor. 12:10.) In fact, it would not be at all inaccurate to translate 1 Corinthians 1:24 as "Christ, the Miracle of God," for in Him is the consummate and ultimate manifestation of the supernatural. Jesus is not only our power, He is our miracle.

Second, *Jesus is our mastery.* Paul told Roman believers, "There is no authority (power) except from God" (Rom. 13:1). John adds, "But as many as received Him, to them He gave the right (or the power) to become children of God, even to those who believe in His name" (John 1:12). The Greek word translated "power" in these texts is *exousia.* The basic meaning relates to one's privilege or rights, but extends from there to encompass a person's influence or sphere of control, including his "mastery" (i.e., his control or authority).

When the disciples said, "What manner of man is this that even the winds and the sea obey Him!" (Matt. 8:27, KJV), they were amazed at the fact that Christ's realm of mastery extended further than they had realized. Later He transferred that very power to His disciples when He said, "I give you the authority to trample on serpents and scorpions, and over all the power of the enemy . . . " (Luke 10:19).

Third, *Jesus is our might*. Two Greek words, *ischus* and *kratos*, describe the sheer strength or might of Christ's power. Paul's second letter to the Thessalonians refers to Christ's coming in the "glory of His power [*ischus*]" (2 Thess. 1:9). This makes it clear that nothing will be able to withstand Him. "Who can endure the day of His coming?" the Old Testament prophet asked (Mal. 3:2). Then, in Revelation, worship is offered to the Lamb, who is worthy to receive "Blessing and honor and glory and power [*kratos*] . . . " (Rev. 5:13). *Kratos* describes the aspect of our Lord's might that is so intense that nothing can withstand it. Although any human illustration would be poor in describing this, one example might be the power of a laser beam. The light of a laser is so concentrated it can penetrate any object. In Christ we discover the concentration of all the power of the Godhead. (See Col. 2:9.) His might is beyond comprehension.

Finally, *Jesus is our magnificence*. Luke tells us that the people who saw Christ cast out a demon were "amazed at the majesty [power] of God" (Luke 9:43). The word here for "power" is *megaleitoes*, which means "magnificence, majesty, or superbness." Here Christ is pictured in His irresistible power, a majestic magnificence that embodies His entire being.

LIVING THIS NAME

To recognize that Christ is not only our miracle, but our mastery, might, and magnificence, gives us great encouragement as we face the uncertainties that lie before us in the hours ahead.

First, *wherever we go, whatever we do, we have the capacity to be a channel for Christ's miracle power.* Whether it's in the miracle of sharing our faith or the miracle of lifting a brother who has fallen, we can watch this day become a day of miracles.

Second, *we can take the mastery of Jesus' name into those situations where Satan seeks to diminish our authority.* We are in control of our day because Christ is in control, and He dwells within us!

Third, *we can face each of today's potential warfare situations rejoicing in the recognition that the might of Christ goes before us into battle.* "The battle is not yours, but God's" (2 Chron. 20:15).

Finally, *we have the joy of living this day saturated with Christ's magnificence.* Through eyes of anticipation we'll see His beauty everywhere—in creation, in circumstances, and even in relationships with others. A hug from a friend, a breath of fresh air, a sunrise or sunset—all will remind us of the magnificence of Jesus.

PRAYING THIS NAME

Because we live in a carnal society that continually seeks to control us with fleshly desires, we need to come boldly before the Lord today claiming His mastery over every temptation.

Honestly tell Him if you've become weary in your warfare. Take time to allow His magnificence to flood your being. And if you face a situation for which only a miracle will do, cry out to God who made this promise: "Call to Me, and I will answer you, and show you great and mighty things, which you do not know" (Jer. 33:3). Then, with Patrick of Ireland, you can boldly pray:

> I bind unto myself today
> the Power of God to hold and lead,
> His eye to watch, His might to stay,
> His ear to hearken to my need.[1]

Especially contend in prayer today for the miracle of personal spiritual restoration. That is the key to mastery in Christ. Petition God as did Martin Luther:

> Behold, Lord, an empty vessel that needs to be filled.
> My Lord, fill it.
> I am weak in the faith; strengthen me.
> I am cold in love; warm me and make me fervent,
> that my love may go out to my neighbor.
> I do not have a strong and firm faith;
> at times I doubt and am unable to trust You altogether.
> O Lord, help me.

Strengthen my faith and trust in You.
In You I have sealed the treasure of all I have.
I am poor; You are rich and came to be merciful to the poor.
I am a sinner; You are upright.
With me there is an abundance of sin;
in You is the fullness of righteousness.
Therefore I will remain with You, of whom I can receive,
but to whom I may not give.[2]

TODAY'S PRAYER

You were the One, Lord Jesus, who said to do it.
"Tarry in Jerusalem until you receive power from on high."
And here I am at Your feet, Lord.
I come to You, the Fountain of power,
and I make your throne room my Jerusalem.
I have come to wait . . . and to receive.
I need Your power, Lord,
but I am slowly learning
that my need and its supply
are different than
I thought.

I thought I needed the ability to do things,
but You wanted to give me the power to become
patient,
understanding,
forgiving,
. . . like You.

I felt I wanted the power to control things,
but You began to teach me that Your power, which
created all things,
sustains all things, and
oversees all things,
is sufficient to manage the issues
that surround and concern me.

So, Lord, I enter a new day of power.
Your day, Your power,
Have become my day and my joy.
Your joy (which I have gained through Your power)

has become my strength.
Hallelujah!
In Jesus' name.
Amen.

HALLOWING THIS NAME

Adonai-Jehovah (Sovereign Lord; Master Jehovah)
—Gen. 15:2, 8 (NIV)
Almighty—Rev. 1:8
Arm of the Lord—Isa. 51:9-10
Christ the Power of God—1 Cor. 1:24
Good Teacher—Mark 10:17
Lord God Almighty—Rev. 4:8
Lord God Omnipotent—Rev. 19:6
Lord Mighty in Battle—Ps. 24:8
Lord Strong and Mighty—Ps. 24:8
Master of the House—Luke 13:25
Mighty God—Isa. 9:6
Mighty One—Ps. 50:1
Mighty One of Israel—Isa. 30:29
Mighty One of Jacob—Isa. 60:16
Most Mighty—Ps. 45:3 (KJV)
My Stength and Power—2 Sam. 22:33
Strong Lord—Ps. 89:8 (KJV)

24
THE WISDOM OF GOD
1 Corinthians 1:24

ENLIGHTENMENT

In his *Sermons,* Fredrick William Faber wrote, "There is hardly ever a complete silence in our soul. God is whispering to us well-nigh incessantly." The scholar concludes, "Whenever the sounds of the world die out in the soul, or sink low, then we hear these whisperings of God. He is always whispering to us, only we do not always hear because of the noise, hurry, and distraction which life causes as it rushes on."[1]

Paul told the Ephesians, "I pray for you constantly, asking God, the glorious Father of our Lord Jesus Christ, to give you *wisdom to see clearly* and *really understand* who Christ is and all that He has done for you" (Eph. 1:16-17, TLB, italics added). Paul was asking God, in Jesus Christ, to give the Ephesians "revelation in the knowledge of Him" (KJV). His intercession further asks that "the eyes of your understanding being enlightened; that you may know what is the hope of His calling, what are the riches of the glory of His inheritance in the saints, and what is the exceeding greatness of His power toward us who believe, according to the working of His mighty power" (Eph. 1:18-19).

God is always longing to enlighten His children concerning Himself, at least to the degree that His children are capable of being enlightened. Phillips Brooks observed: "Remember, God is teaching you always just as much truth as you can learn. If you are in sorrow at your ignorance, then . . . you must not despair. Be capable of more knowledge and it shall be given to you."[2]

Why does God reveal Himself as He does? William Law in *A Serious Call to a Devout and Holy Life* aptly answers, "God ordains a revelation in this or that manner, time, and place, not because it is a justice that He cannot refuse, not because it is a matter of favor or free goodness, and therefore may be given in any manner at pleasure, but because He has the whole race of mankind, the whole order of human changes and events, the whole combination of all cause and effects of human tempers, all the actions of free agents, and all the consequences of every revelation, plainly in His sight."[3]

God truly knows more than we will ever know, and His ways are clearly above our ways (Isa. 55:8). He is infinite in wisdom and knowledge and has chosen to reveal all His wisdom through the person of His Son, Jesus Christ, whom Paul pictures as the Wisdom of God.

KNOWING THIS NAME

Paul not only introduces Jesus to us as the Power of God (1 Cor. 1:24) but in the next breath he calls Him "the Wisdom of God." Six verses later the apostle tells us Christ is "made unto us" or "became for us" wisdom from God. The Greek word used here for wisdom is *sophia*. Christ is not just wisdom; He is the Wisdom of God. All other efforts at illumination are philosophies and sophisticated efforts of man to obtain wisdom, which always end up deficient. This is because true wisdom comes only from the originator of wisdom, the Creator Himself. That's why the author of Proverbs links all wisdom to God with such statements as, "The fear of the Lord is the beginning of wisdom" (Prov. 9:10). *The Living Bible* paraphrases this: "The reverence and fear of God are basic to all wisdom." Only the Creator can create wisdom, and in Christ He not only sent wisdom to us, but He caused Christ to become wisdom *in* us.

Wisdom and knowledge, of course, are not the same. Knowledge is the comprehension or informational side of a matter, whereas wisdom is the practical or operational side of it. Wisdom is knowing how to do what needs to be done. It is the insight into making something work properly, to making it functional.

A sad deficiency of so much of today's information-based society is that people know what they want to do, and even what they ought to do, but they don't know how to do it in such a way as to "make life work." But in Jesus' name as the Wisdom of God we discover Christ is our "resource of wisdom" who will make life work. He'll show us how to make the details of the day (and the primary issues of our lives) function smoothly and properly.

To impart this wisdom Christ has given us His Holy Spirit, the agent of all divine revelation (2 Pet. 1:20-21). "He will teach you all things," Jesus told us (John 14:26). Paul later prayed, "That the God of our Lord Jesus Christ . . . may give to you the spirit of wisdom and revelation in the knowledge of Him, the eyes of your understanding being enlightened . . . " (Eph. 1:17-18). To the Colossians Paul wrote, " In (Christ) are hidden all the treasures of wisdom and knowledge" (Col. 2:3), treasures only revealed by the operations of the Spirit of wisdom, God's Holy Spirit.

LIVING THIS NAME

Because wisdom means "the right use of knowledge," to live today in Jesus' name, the Wisdom of God, is to approach this day trusting Christ's presence to help us apply what we've already learned in Him. Naturally to do this we must know the promises of God as revealed in His Word. So spending time in God's Word every day is essential to living effectively in Jesus' name.

Note also the many times in Scripture that the Bible suggests that we're not merely to read God's promises, we're to live in them (Deut. 6:6-9; 7:11-15; 28:1-2; 29:9). Even our meditation in the Word is to continue "day and night" (Josh. 1:8; Ps. 1:2).

We might also anticipate those occasions when God will speak His miraculous wisdom into situations "by His Spirit." Paul referred to this manifestation (gifts) of the Spirit as "the word of wisdom" (1 Cor. 12:7-8).

Equally exciting is the way the psalmist pictures God's creative acts as expressions of His wisdom. God knows how to bring things which presently do not exist into being. We read, "O Lord, how manifold are Your works, *in wisdom* You have made them all" (Ps. 104:24, italics added). Note also, "To Him who by wisdom made the heavens . . . who laid out the earth above the waters . . ." (Ps. 136:5-6). This suggests that in Christ, who is the

Wisdom of God, we will discover the creative power of God, which literally functions moment-by-moment through us as we live in Jesus' name!

PRAYING THIS NAME

You've probably discovered by now that many names and titles of Christ in Scripture appear similar and seem interchangeable. Christ, for example, is our Wonderful Counselor, providing daily insight; our Great Light, giving daily guidance; and the Wisdom of God, ever enlightening us in His Word. This similarity should not surprise us since Jesus is always everything that all His names and titles picture Him to be. He is our entire list (and more) on any given day. We've only assigned different topics to different days to assist us in grasping the vastness of the facets of His total person.

Today we are highlighting our need for enlightenment through the pages of God's Word, something essential for every day if we're to pray effectively in Jesus' name. We cannot live the Word, apply the Word, pray the Word, know the Word, or even spread the Word if we do not first read the Word. And our capacity to apply the Word effectively will be equal to our willingness to wait long enough in the Word for the Holy Spirit to come and enlighten our minds in its promises.

So take God's Word today and make it a primary part of your praying. As you hold the pages open before you, you might wish to pray what John Calvin often prayed before embarking on his daily journey in God's Word:

> O Lord, heavenly Father, in whom is the
> fullness of light and wisdom,
> Enlighten my mind by Your Holy Spirit,
> And give me grace to receive Your Word with
> reverence and humility,
> Without which no one can understand Your truth.
> For Christ's sake, amen.[4]

TODAY'S PRAYER

It is comforting, Father,
so inspiring to my faith to read Your Word, which says,

"If any of you lacks wisdom, let him ask of God,
who gives to all liberally and without reproach,
and it will be given to him" (James 1:5).
You knew it all along, of course,
that more than anything, other than forgiveness,
we needed wisdom.

You underscored in Your Word how appropriate it was that
Solomon, having the choice of asking anything he wished,
asked for wisdom rather than riches.

Now, as I come before You today, Lord,
I feel very unlike Solomon.
I am too inclined to seek a shortcut to solutions.
I am too quick to suppose easy answers are forthcoming.
But I'm here to make the one request
You've taught me for such situations:
"Ask in faith (for wisdom), nothing doubting."
And I'm encouraged to believe—in fact, Father, I do—
I do believe You are ready this moment to give me
wisdom for today,
wisdom for its decisions,
wisdom for my conversations, and
wisdom for touching others with Your love.
And the reason I do believe is not only because You have
said You will give freely to those who ask,
but because You have made Jesus to become
wisdom for me and unto me.
And it is in His name I pray.
Amen.

HALLOWING THIS NAME
Chief Shepherd—1 Pet. 5:4
Counselor—Isa. 9:6
Faithful and True Witness—Rev. 3:14
Faithful Witness—Rev. 1:5
Good Teacher—Mark 10:17
Great Light—Isa. 9:2
Habitation of Justice—Jer. 50:7
Lawgiver—Isa. 33:22
Master—Matt. 23:8 (KJV)

Messiah—John 4:25
My Lamp—2 Sam. 22:29
Only Wise God—1 Tim. 1:17 (KJV)
Rabbi—John 1:49
Spirit of Justice—Isa. 28:5-6
Wisdom—Prov. 8:12
Word—1 John 1:1
Word of God—Rev. 19:13
Word of Life—1 John 1:1

25
THE WAY, THE TRUTH, AND THE LIFE
John 14:6

PURPOSE

When the old man who was considered the town sloth came to Christ in a revival meeting, acquaintances wondered if his conversion would correct his laziness or if "putting off the old man" would require some extra effort in the days ahead. Their answer came the following week when the new convert prayed his first public prayer at the midweek prayer meeting: "Use me, Lord, use me—in an advisory capacity!"

But God isn't looking for servants to assist Him in an advisory capacity. He has an eternal purpose for all who would respond in obedience to his call to service. Through Jeremiah God said, "For I know the plans I have for you. . . . They are plans for good and not for evil, to give you a future and a hope" (Jer. 29:11, TLB).

Here is a promise of purpose. And this purpose is not found in a cause or a creed but a person, our Lord Jesus Christ, who describes Himself as "the Way, the Truth, and the Life" (John 14:6).

KNOWING THIS NAME

In *Harvest Time* Charles Spurgeon stated: "The world is just a materializing of God's thoughts, for the world is a thought in

God's eyes. He made it first from a thought that came from His own mighty hand, and everything in this majestic temple He has made has a meaning."[1] Joseph Hall in *The Pleasures of Study* adds, "How endless is that volume which God has written of the world! Wherein every creature is a letter, every day a new page."[2]

You are important to God, a page on which God longs to inscribe, in the very signature of His Son, a prescription for a life of purpose. And that life of purpose begins with a recognition that Christ, alone, is the Way, the Truth, and the Life (John 14:6). Although each of these terms might be defined separately, Christ uses them in reference to Himself in a single statement. It is a statement best defined by the single word *purpose.*

"The Way," the first title on the list, comes from the Greek *hodos* and is used in a variety of ways in both the New Testament and Greek literature. It can refer to a narrow path beaten out by those who've gone before, or a broad road made for chariot traffic. It also was used to describe highways ("troop trails") on which soldiers would march to battle or hold great ceremonial processions. *Hodos* also was used to describe the route taken by a ship or the course taken by a river (riverbed). In fact, everything from a major roadway to a tiny footpath is encompassed in this word.

Taken as a whole, Christ as our Way suggests someone who is with us in every tight place (narrow path), tempting place (broad road), deep waters, or even wilderness experiences (those dry riverbeds). No matter where we are, the Way is with us! More specifically, when Christ pictured Himself as the Way, He was describing Himself as the One who provides supportive footing for our approach to God as well as assurance that we are moving in the right direction. As the Way, Christ also serves as our ever-present guide, stationed at every point en route to God's purposes for His children.

Thomas à Kempis found the Way and sought with all his might to imitate Him. His immortal *The Imitation of Christ* is perhaps the most widely read devotional Christian book in history. Kempis wrote:

> I am the Way, the Truth, and the Life,
> Without the Way there is no going;
> Without the Truth there is no knowing;
> Without the Life there is no living.
> I am the Way which thou shouldst pursue;

I am the Truth which thou shouldst believe;
I am the Life which thou shouldst hope for.

Christ further pictures Himself as the Truth. Bible commentator Herbert Lockyer suggests that Jesus qualifies as the Truth because He could not lie. He is the sum total of the truth He taught, He is the guarantee for fulfilled promises, and He reveals truth to every phase of life.[3] In practical terms this suggests that by living in Jesus as the Truth I am assisted against compromising my integrity. I have the totality of truth dwelling within me to face life's many demands. I have a living guarantee that His promises to me cannot fail and each situation and phase of life will have validity and meaning. Simply stated, Christ is the Way to navigate life's pathways—and that's the truth!

Concerning the final expression on our list, the Life, the Greek language employs two words, *zoe* and *bios*, from which we derive the words *zoology* and *biology* respectively. There is a distinct contrast in the usage of these two words in the New Testament. *Bios* relates to man's existence, whereas *zoe* (used in John 14:6) relates to his purpose and destiny. *Bios* concerns the essential functions of the human being, whereas *zoe* concerns the spiritual and moral qualities of life. Jesus is the Zoe—the highest expression and intent of life. And although man shares *bios* features with the animal realm or kingdom, he is designed to know *zoe* in an eternal and abundant dimension. The Bible says, "He who has the Son has life *[Zoe]*; he who does not have the Son of God does not have life *[Zoe]*" (1 John 5:11-12).

LIVING THIS NAME

Man is special in God's eyes; a creature made "with purpose" to be possessed by the Zoe, Christ Himself. All of earth was designed to prepare man for this purpose. Henry Ward Beecher said in *Royal Truth*, "When God wanted sponges and oysters, He made them, and put one on a rock and the other in the mud. When He made man, He didn't make him to be a sponge or an oyster; He made him with feet and hands, and head and heart, and vital blood, and a place to use them, and He said to him, 'Go, work!' "[4]

To live in Jesus' name, the Way, the Truth, and the Life, is to tap into Christ's Zoe-power in every task we undertake. Nothing must be left to chance. Paul told the Corinthians, "I run straight to the goal with purpose in every step" (1 Cor. 9:26, TLB). Today's goal must be to find God's plan and purpose for all we experience and declare His name as we move into each task. We can take His purposes into family situations, personal relationships, business appointments, and other potentially demanding or even stressful circumstances. We can fill this day, in Jesus' name, with purpose.

PRAYING THIS NAME

Three centuries ago Bishop Stratford prayed, "O Lord, let me not live to be useless."[5] Christ longs to release usefulness into every day we live. And daily prayer is the place where a true usefulness with purpose begins.

To pray in Jesus' name, the Way, the Truth, and the Life, is to speak purpose into your day. With boldness you can offer today's petitions knowing you have found the Way, you know the Truth, and you're filled with Life. Your day counts because you have brought God's purpose into it through prayer.

More specifically, you can claim Christ's way for today concerning purpose and direction for your family, friends, or even government officials. Then you can pray for Christ's truth to flow into circumstances where Satan as the father of lies would seek to sow deeper seeds of deception and untruth. Finally, you can speak Christ's Zoe-power into all areas of potential conflict, areas where something of a cloud of death hangs as a mockery to continual health and happiness. Jesus' name means life—abundant life—and you can saturate your prayers with the fullness of that life!

Praise God for the delight you can have today in drawing near to God in Jesus' name. How can you be defeated? The Way will guide you, the Truth will guard you, and the Life will undergird you in all you do! Joyfully you can join Desiderius Erasmus in his prayer:

> O Lord Jesus Christ,
> You have said that You are the Way,
> the Truth, and the Life.
> Suffer us not to stray from You, who are the Way,
> Not to distrust You, who are the Truth,
> Nor to rest in anything other than You,
> who are the Life![6]

TODAY'S PRAYER

Lord Jesus Christ,
I come to You today as the Way, the Truth and the Life.
My prayer is that You would become
my Way, my Truth, and my Life.
I don't mean that I want You to conform to me,
but precisely the opposite.
I want to walk my steps in Your Way.
I want to think my thoughts in Your Truth.
I want my experience to be of Your Life.

Lord, may I ask that this take place at least one day.
If I can taste the fulfillment of that for this one day,
I know I'll not only desire it all the more tomorrow, but I'll
be all the more confident it can happen again . . .
And again . . . and again.

Dear Jesus, I need daily
direction as to what to do,
instruction as to how to do it, and
inspiration to give me ability for the doing of it.
So it fills me with joy in anticipating that You,
the Way (giving direction), and
the Truth (giving instruction), and
the Life (giving inspiration),
have made Yourself fully available
to be all of that
to me, for me and in me.
Thank You, Lord.
In Jesus' name.
Amen.

HALLOWING THIS NAME

Apostle of Our Profession—Heb. 3:1
Christ Our Life—Col. 3:4
God of Justice—Isa. 30:18
God of My Life—Ps. 42:8
God of Truth—Deut. 32:4
Good—Ps. 34:8
Great Prophet—Luke 7:16

He Who Lives—Rev. 1:18
Just One—Acts 7:52
Lord God of Truth—Ps. 31:5
My Lamp—2 Sam. 22:29
My Righteous Servant—Isa. 53:11
Prince of Life—Acts 3:15
Resurrection and the Life—John 11:25
True Light—John 1:9

26
THE DELIVERER
Romans 11:26

LIBERATION

A Welsh preacher approached his pulpit and began his morning sermon: "Friends, I have a question to ask. I cannot answer it. You cannot answer it. If an angel from heaven were here, he could not answer it. If a devil from hell were here, he could not answer it."

The entire congregation waited anxiously for the preacher's next words. Then, after a longer than usual pause, he added, "The question is: 'How shall we escape if we neglect so great a salvation?' " (Heb. 2:3).

Jesus is our Deliverer, so to neglect Christ as Savior is to neglect our only means of deliverance. Sadly, many neglect their only hope of liberation, thereby distancing themselves from deliverance. In *Gnomologia* Thomas Fuller wisely observed, "He that has led a wicked life is afraid of his own memory."[1]

It is Christ the Deliverer who liberates us from the bondage of sin and brings us to a full realization of the power of God's holiness. And as Charles Spurgeon wrote, "Holiness is the architectural plan upon which God buildeth up His living temple."

KNOWING THIS NAME

Paul introduces us to Christ the Deliverer in Romans 11:26. His reference is actually a quotation from Psalm 14:6, which is later quoted by Isaiah (59:20). The psalmist's reference is one of assurance that no matter the degree of attack upon the believer from his enemies, the Lord will bring deliverance. The Isaiah passage, which uses the title "Redeemer" in reference to our Messiah, is the one specifically alluded to by Paul when he said: "This is My covenant with them, when I take away their sins." Here we have an oath, a covenant-agreement, taken by God that declares once we become His, He will become our Deliverer (or Redeemer) and will "take away" our sins.

Looking more closely at this reality, numerous aspects of our Deliverer's work may be found in a variety of Scriptures.

First, *we note that Christ delivers us from "this body of death."* This is a reference to the craving of our carnal, fleshly nature which yearns to have its own way (Rom. 7:24).

Second, *Christ delivers us out of "the hand of our enemies"* (Luke 1:74). The psalmist identifies our enemies as "many" who would "daily" swallow us up (Ps. 56:2, KJV).

Third, *Christ delivers from "the mouth of the lion"* (2 Tim. 4:17). Here Jesus is pictured as our New Testament equivalent to Daniel's deliverer. Our adversary roars about as a lion seeking whom he may devour, but in Christ we have a Deliverer. We recall how Daniel seemed beyond hope in the lions' den, yet King Darius, who puts him there in the first place, repeatedly affirmed that the Lord would be Daniel's deliverer (see Dan. 7:16, 20, 27).

Finally, *Christ will deliver us from "the wrath to come"* as Paul *instructed the Thessalonians* (1 Thess. 1:10). In Jesus' name we rest in the hope that Christ's coming and His catching us away before earth's darkest hour will mark our ultimate deliverance in Him as our Deliverer.

The Greek word for "deliver" in all of these passages is *rumoai,* meaning "to rescue, save, deliver, preserve, or liberate." It is worthwhile to note the ways this word is used in Homeric literature such as *The Odyssey.* There we discover Odysseus' inability to save *(rumoai)* any of his men who, in the eyes of their various gods, were guilty and beyond salvation. Similarly, the gods themselves were unable to save *(rumoai)* any human being beyond the limits of his own destiny. But, hallelujah, in Christ we have a Deliverer who can save us in spite of our guilt. He is a God who brings us into an exciting new destiny through the deliverance that Christ alone can bring. Paul wrote, "If anyone is in Christ, he is a new creation" (2 Cor. 5:17). This implies an all-new destiny. Our former "destined" failure is now overruled by something altogether new.

Our English word *deliver* also merits evaluation. It opens before us as a multiple set of insights that greatly expands the significance of the title of Deliverer. The word *deliver* means:

- to set free or save from evil or danger;
- to assist a woman at the birth of an offspring;
- to give forth or express in words, as in delivering a speech or announcement;
- to give, hand over, transfer or carry to and leave at the proper place or places;
- to give or send forth (such as an oil well delivers twenty barrels a day); and
- to strike a blow, as in "delivering a punch."

These possibilities unlock a richer understanding of the many ways Christ serves as our Deliverer. They also help us better appreciate the beautiful hymn:

'Tis the grandest theme through the ages wrung,
'Tis the grandest theme on immortal tongue,
'Tis the grandest theme that the world has sung,
Our God is able to deliver thee![2]

LIVING THIS NAME

To live today in Jesus' name, our Deliverer, is to approach each circumstance in the liberating power of Christ's presence. What is there in you that needs liberating today? Does anger often affect your day? Do lustful thoughts trouble you? Has cheating become so commonplace that you hardly realize you're doing it anymore?

Picture yourself confronting each temptation, one at a time, but not alone—Jesus is beside you in each battle.

And as you move into this day with Christ your Deliverer beside you, take heart in the recognition that your deliverance is a multifaceted, never-ending work of Christ. The Bible tells us Christ "delivered us from so great a death, and is presently delivering us, and we trust Him to yet be delivering us in the future" (2 Cor. 1:10, personal paraphrase). True, we all receive a certain deliverance from sin's past penalty the instant we are saved. But there is likewise a growing or continuing deliverance from sin's present power (in our flesh), which we progressively realize through our growth in Christ.

And there is an ultimate deliverance from sin's future presence that we shall realize only when we meet Christ. Thus, our deliverance is complete: past, present, and future.

Think of the implications this has for your day. Your Deliverer not only is with you, He has gone before you into the circumstances that would normally cause you to yield in the face of temptation. You've not only been delivered from your past, but deliverance-power is right now working liberation in your present. Best of all, in Jesus' name you need not fear failure in your future for your Deliverer is already there, laying the groundwork for your future liberation.

PRAYING THIS NAME

As you pray today in Jesus' name, your Deliverer, pray through the list of definitions given earlier for "deliver."

First, *"deliver" means to set free or save from evil or danger.* Can you think of a circumstance in which "freedom" or "deliverance" is needed, perhaps by a friend or loved one facing evil or danger? Contend for deliverance in that situation in Jesus' name.

Second, *"deliver" means to assist a woman at the birth of an offspring.* Is there something God has promised to "birth" or bring into existence in or through your life that is not yet a reality? Could this be God's time to deliver on that promise? You may wish to ask Him for a spirit of travail to help you "push forth" that victory from the womb of the invisible into the realm of reality.

Third, *"deliver" means to give forth or express in words, as in delivering a speech.* Is it time today to deliver that witness of Christ's love to your boss, family member, or friend whom you've never been able to approach about the salvation experience? Claim Christ's deliverance-power now for a victory before this day passes.

Fourth, *"deliver" means to give, hand over, or transfer, as in delivering a message.* Could it be that God would use you today to deliver a special word from Him to one of His choice warriors who has become weary in His warfare?

Fifth, *"deliver" means to send forth, such as a well delivers oil or water.* "That employee really delivers" is how an employer often describes someone who is hard-working. In this sense, God desires that His children deliver in all they do: "Whatever your hand finds to do, do it with your might" (Eccl. 9:10).

Finally, *"deliver" means to strike a blow, as in "delivering a punch."* Beloved, let's use our time of prayer today in Jesus' name to send some blows in Satan's direction. Armed with God's Word, take a few swings even now. As you do so, remember: He who praises most swings best! Nothing seems to anger Satan more than a believer's worship of the most high God. Why not take a few more swings?

TODAY'S PRAYER

Once in all hist'ry, O great the myst'ry
God came to earth veiled in flesh so man could see.
In Christ the Savior, God showed His favor—
He to redeem us ascended Calvary.
Dark was the hour, hell-born the power
Which tore the flesh of the Lamb spent on the Tree.
Death now partaking—Hell's power breaking—
Hear "It is finished!" The Lamb cries, "Victory!"
Come to the Mountain—Bathe in the Fountain,
Wash in the Blood Jesus shed upon that Cross.
Call Jesus' name now—come make your claim now,
He'll break your bondage; redeem your every loss.
Great deliverance, mighty redemption
That can reach the lost like me,
Cleanse from guilt and set me free.
So I'll shout, "Hallelujah!"
And, "Praise God—Jehovah!"
For that great deliverance and great victory.

J.W.H.

Dear Lord,
I pray as You taught me to,
"Deliver me from evil."
I pray as David prayed,
"Search me and know me
and see if there be some wicked way in me,
and lead me in the Way everlasting."

I pray that You would break the yoke
of anything other than Your soul-yoke,
which makes me Your disciple,
Your servant, and Your friend.

Let the anointing of Your Holy Spirit
break my every bond and set my spirit free
to serve Your holy purpose and worship Your holy name—
My Deliverer, Mighty Jesus!
In Your name.
Amen.

HALLOWING THIS NAME

Advocate—1 John 2:1
Angel of His Presence—Isa. 63:9
Author of Eternal Salvation—Heb. 5:9
Branch of Righteousness—Jer. 23:5
Door of the Sheep—John 10:7
Eternal Life—1 John 5:20
Firstborn from the Dead—Rev. 1:5
God My Savior—Luke 1:47
Horn of Salvation—Luke 1:69
Lamb without Blemish—1 Pet. 1:19
Man of Sorrows—Isa. 53:3
Man of War—Exod. 15:3
Messenger of the Covenant—Mal. 3:1
Ransom—Mark 10:45
Redeemer—Isa. 59:20
Savior of the World—1 John 4:14
Son of Mary—Mark 6:3
Testator—Heb. 9:16
Tower of Salvation—2 Sam. 22:51

27

THE LORD OF GLORY
1 Corinthians 2:7-8

MAJESTY

Creation is a reflection of its Creator and all the beauty about us mirrors the majesty of God. Whether a snowflake being probed under the eye of a microscope or a galaxy being studied through the lens of a telescope, all of creation testifies to the splendor of Christ's "mantle of majesty."

Of this mantle the psalmist said, "The heavens declare the glory of God; and the firmament shows His handiwork" (Ps. 19:1); and, "The Lord reigns, He is clothed with majesty" (Ps. 93:1).

To say our Lord is clothed with majesty is to say that all creation is "window dressing" for Christ's excellence. It all points to Him. And just as a king's palace with all its royal decor reflects something of the nature of that king's personality, so creation reflects the magnificence of our Lord's nature and character.

But more amazing is the fact that God, who was clothed with majesty, chose to become the personification of majesty when He came to earth in the form of His Son, Jesus Christ. Paul wrote, "God was in Christ reconciling the world to Himself . . ." (2 Cor. 5:19, NEB). It is in this regard that we can say Christ is the ultimate essence of God's glory and the personification of His immeasurable majesty. Christ, alone, is the majesty of God wrapped up in a person.

157

KNOWING THIS NAME

Paul sums up this reality in referring to Christ as the Lord of Glory (1 Cor. 2:7-8). Although the concept of this word *glory* is that of excellence, in 1 Corinthians 2:8 Paul pictures Christ as the consummate "excellent one," who excels all His creation. Jesus is not merely excellence, he's the Lord of Excellence. Clearly this is a reference to Christ's royalty as well as His splendor.

The Greek word *doxa* (from which we derive doxology) initially concerns brightness and radiance. We especially see this in 1 Corinthians 15:40 where *doxa* refers to the varied degrees of the magnitude and brightness ("glory") of the stars and moon.

The sheer brilliance of Christ's majesty is really an outflow of the expression of Christ Himself as God. Scripture states, "God is light and in Him is no darkness at all" (1 John 1:5) and Christ dwells in "unapproachable light" (1 Tim. 6:16).

The amazing thing about our text (1 Cor. 2:7-8) is that it focuses our attention on the marvelous wisdom by which Christ covered Himself, or hid His glory. In doing this, the powers of hell and of this world did not realize that this Man, who appeared so weak, so without majesty as He humbled Himself on the Cross, was in fact the Lord of Glory—the One "excelling" all! Further, according to our text, it is by this action that, wonder of wonders, Christ was accomplishing an act that would be for our glory (v. 7). Indeed, Christ hid His very manifest glory in order to make us partakers in His excellence.

Now note the tender and significant statement in Christ's high priestly prayer where He specifically asks: "Father, I desire that they also whom You gave Me may be with Me where I am, that they may behold My glory which You have given Me; for You loved Me before the foundation of the world" (John 17:24).

Here Jesus acknowledges two essential facts. First, His longing that we might understand the splendor of His person and so more fully appreciate the marvel of the love that compelled Him to lay aside this glory and splendor to come to us. Second, His desire that we share in that glory with Him, regardless of our position in society. Hebrews 2:10 emphasizes this goal in Christ's reference to "bringing many sons unto glory." Here we see a love that begins as He causes us to be "raised up together" with Christ and made to "sit together in the heavenly places in Christ Jesus," and which continues timelessly, "that in the ages to come He might show the exceeding riches of His grace in His kindness toward us in Christ Jesus" (Eph. 2:6-7).

It's especially significant to note that the second and only other place in the New Testament where Christ is referred to as the Lord of Glory is in a passage that speaks against showing partiality toward people according to their social status. In James 2:1 we read, "My brethren, do not hold the faith of our Lord Jesus Christ, *the Lord of glory* (literally "the Glorious One"), with partiality" (italics added). The passage suggests that we are to be as indiscriminate as Christ was when He sacrificed His life for all the "whoevers" of this world (John 3:16; Rom. 10:13). He has invited us all to be equal sharers with Him in His glory. Therefore as a community of believers we are not to distinguish between different levels of earthly glory at the expense of any who lack special graces, gifts, or resources.

Chabod, the Old Testament Hebrew word for "glory," focuses more on the idea of weightiness than brightness. Here the concept of worth or worthiness is related to weight—as with scales measuring the value of precious materials or stones—rather than on how brightly these metals or gems shine. "The Glory of the Lord," in this sense, then, is in the weight of His worth, and by His very nature He literally outweighs any value or force compared or opposed to Him.

Thus, all our burdens, transferred unto Him, are as nothing to Him. All our sins, for we have been weighed and found wanting, are outweighed by His glorious majesty demonstrated in His death for us. Further, in any contest, like that of a boxer or wrestler in a ring, the Lord "outweighs" our every opponent. No enemy can withstand the force of Christ's person or the glory of His greatness as we take our stand in Him.

This idea of weight helps us understand 2 Corinthians 4:17 which reminds us that the burdens (weights) of this life are not worthy to be compared to the "glory which shall be revealed in us" (Rom. 8:18). In the end it will work for us "a far more exceeding and eternal weight of glory" (2 Cor. 4:17).

LIVING THIS NAME

Much attention has been given in this chapter to the idea of glory as it relates to our overall theme, the Lord of Glory. We should not, however, overlook the important fact that Jesus is not merely

159

our glory (even our glory personified), He is the Lord of that glory. And because glory is excellence, this combination of terms suggests that Christ is the Lord of our excellence.

What do we mean when we use the term *Lord* in reference to Christ? And how does an understanding of this expression help us live today in Jesus' name with greater authority?

For one thing, the word *Lord* (the Greek *kurios*) not only means "master" but "owner." The word *master* suggests "one to whom service is due on any ground" and *owner* includes "one who has the disposal or control of anything." Jesus is more than merely the "Master" of God's glory (excellence), He is the "Owner" of that excellence. Christ has at His disposal all that is excellent.

Thus, to live in Jesus' name, the Lord [owner and master] of Glory, is to conduct all our business in the recognition that Christ is our excellence and majesty. All the glory of this day is His. All recognition we may receive for any accomplishments really belongs to Him. And we should declare God's glory throughout our day. Spoken praise need not cease when we exit the prayer closet. Since the majesty of our Lord is everywhere, our praises can be offered anywhere.

PRAYING THIS NAME

Because our Lord is clothed with His splendor (that is, His glory), to pray in Jesus' name, the Lord of Glory, is to saturate ourselves with His excellence and majesty in prayer. Paul told Roman believers: "Put on the Lord Jesus Christ" (Rom. 13:14). We should be careful not to leave our dwelling today until we're "dressed up" in Jesus. Look at the list of some of the names of Jesus and prayerfully put them on! Tell the Lord you've chosen to wear His provision today, or His excellence, boldness, comfort, or confidence— or whatever else your day might require.

Remember, Jesus is always all of these qualities, and many more, but in declaring them afresh, your trust increases. As the psalmist reminded us, "Those who know Your name will put their trust in You" (Ps. 9:10).

Also take a moment to declare Christ your owner and master in all you do today. Identify a circumstance or situation and simply say, "Jesus, I declare You to be Owner of that circumstance," or, "Lord, I proclaim You are Master in this situation."

Finally, to pray in Jesus' name, the Lord of Glory, is to speak His majesty, His royalty, and His eternal excellence into the details, decisions, and desires of the day. It is to linger long enough with Jesus to catch some of the glow of His glory and thereby radiate His presence throughout the day. It is to be, as Christ's disciples were, "eye-witnesses of His majesty" (2 Pet. 1:16, NIV).

TODAY'S PRAYER

Dear Father,
I come with thanksgiving today because You sent Jesus
as a light to shine in the darkness of this world.
I praise You for the substance—the sheer weight of glory—
that pours into each soul and every situation
that opens to His light.

Today I want to live in His name—he who is the Lord of Glory.
I want Christ's radiance to brighten my countenance,
that I might bring the light of joy to people
who are living in the shadows of difficulty;
May Christ's light spill over the brim of my life
in such a way that people capture a sense of Your warmth
without my having to seem or sound "religious";
and may the weight—
the genuine "heavy-weight" reality of Christ's character—
be increased in me.
Let the stamp of His
personality be left where I have been.
In His name.
Amen.

HALLOWING THIS NAME

Blessed and Only Potentate—1 Tim. 6:15
Chiefest among Ten Thousand—Song of Sol. 5:10
Crown of Glory—Isa. 28:5
Diadem of Beauty—Isa. 28:5
Glorious Throne to His Father's House—Isa. 22:23
God of Glory—Acts 7:2
Great King above All Gods—Ps. 95:3
High and Lofty One—Isa. 57:15
Highest—Luke 1:76

Hope of Glory—Col. 1:27
Jehovah-Elyon (The Lord Most High)—Ps. 7:17
King—Zech. 14:16
King in His Beauty—Isa. 33:17
King of Glory—Ps. 24:7, 10
King of Israel—John 1:49
King of Jacob—Isa. 41:21
King of Kings—Rev. 17:14
King of Saints—Rev. 15:3
King Over All the Earth—Zech. 14:9
Lily of the Valley—Song of Sol. 2:1
Lord and Savior Jesus Christ—2 Pet. 3:18
Lord from Heaven—1 Cor. 15:47
Lord Most High—Ps. 47:2
Lord of Lords—Rev. 17:14
Lord—Rom. 10:13
Majestic Lord—Isa. 33:21
Most High—Ps. 18:13
Prince and Savior—Acts 5:30-31
Prince of Princes—Dan. 8:25
Righteous Judge—2 Tim. 4:8
Rose of Sharon—Song of Sol. 2:1
Ruler over the Kings of the Earth—Rev. 1:5
Sharp Sword—Isa. 49:2
Son—1 John 4:14
Your King—Zech. 9:9

28
THE BREAD OF LIFE
John 6:35

NOURISHMENT

A particular feature of Japanese horticulture is the unique cultivation of dwarf trees. These are exact duplicates, which the Japanese grow in flower pots, of the giant trees that grow unhindered in the forests. These dwarf trees are true trees—some more than a century old—yet they grow only two or three feet tall. These trees possess all the features of a full grown tree and appear exactly as a forest tree would if viewed through the wrong end of binoculars.

The Japanese gardener takes great pains in growing these miniature trees. They are raised from seeds, and the gardener takes various steps to suppress growth when the trees are only a few inches high. In order to starve and cripple the trees, they are transplanted to pots that do not contain enough soil to nourish their branches. If buds appear, they are removed. Eventually the trees put forth no new buds and remain dwarfs throughout life.

So it is with spiritual dwarfs, those in Christ's body who never mature in Jesus. Surveys on the frequency of devotional habits among God's people usually reveal some frightening facts. According to a radio evangelist, one survey involving fifteen hundred lay Christians and pastors indicated the average believer spent only sixty seconds a day in a specific quiet time, excluding time for saying grace at mealtime. Leaders didn't fare much better—they spent an average of only ninety seconds a day in devotional prayer.

Little wonder the church is so weak in the face of an unholy world. Missionary statesman E. Stanley Jones said, "I am better or worse as I pray more or less. It works for me with mathematical precision."

Christ said it thus, "Man shall not live by bread alone, but by every word that proceeds from the mouth of God" (Matt. 4:4). Loosely paraphrased, this might read—"No nourishment, no growth; no food, no fruit!"

KNOWING THIS NAME

John, who provides us with a variety of views regarding Christ's character through His names and titles, also introduces us to Jesus as the Bread of Life 6:35). The context of this revelation includes Christ's introduction of what we traditionally call the Lord's Table (John 6:53-58). Early in the chapter we are told the Passover was near, a fact that sets the tone for Christ's instruction. He intended to convey that He is the nourishing equivalent of the Passover lamb, just as surely as He is its redemptive equivalent. Not only did the blood of the Passover lamb protect God's people (Exod. 12:7, 13), and in that sense save them, but the Lamb nourished them as well (Exod. 12:8). But now Christ's disciples seem puzzled as their Lord says pointedly, "For My flesh is food indeed, and My blood is drink indeed" (John 6:55).

Jesus goes on to explain that He is teaching a spiritual truth (v. 63) which is foreshadowed in the Exodus account (Exod. 12). There, the Passover is pictured as providing protection. The blood of the lamb placed upon the two doorposts and on the lintel of the door established their faith-filled response to God's promise: "When I see the blood, I will pass over you" (v. 13). But the people were likewise directed to eat the lamb (vv. 8-10) for strength for the journey that would immediately follow their deliverance. And in John 6:35 Christ presents Himself as providing both nourishment and deliverance. Now we discover Jesus is both the Lamb of God and the Bread of Life. We not only need to be saved, we need to be sustained.

LIVING THIS NAME

There are numerous mentions of bread in the Bible that give us insight into what it means to live daily in Jesus' name, the Bread of Life. The Genesis account of man's fall is one example. It explains that because of the curse of sin man would be required to earn his bread or sustenance by the sweat of his brow (Gen. 3:19). But in Christ, who is our "living bread," salvation is freely given. We don't have to earn it; salvation is a gift (Eph. 2:8). This suggests that living today in Jesus' name, the Bread of Life, is to live in the fullness of Christ as our Savior.

Later in Genesis we read of Joseph's management of the grain (bread) during Egypt's famine and his loving care for his brethren as the famine reaches them (Gen. 41). Here again we see a picture of Jesus, this time as our Sustainer. As the Bread of Life, He is able to sustain us in times of deficiency.

Then in the early verses of our text for this study (John 6), we find the account of Jesus feeding the multitude out of a very limited supply. As the Bread of Life, Christ is never disabled by the limitations of a circumstance. No matter how insignificant a resource may seem, He is able to multiply it fully to the meeting of our every need. He is our Supplier.

PRAYING THIS NAME

Christ refers to Himself as "bread" ten times in John's Gospel. On one of those occasions He specifically likens Himself to the manna Israel fed upon in the wilderness. (Compare John 6:32 and Exod. 16:4.) In looking back to the Exodus lesson of God's gift of manna, we discover several unique insights that help us pray in Jesus' name, the Bread of Life.

First, *there was a fresh supply of heaven's nourishment available daily* (Exod. 16:4). Nothing God has prepared for us is stale. Scriptures that we read today may have been written centuries ago, but in Jesus' name they will come alive with new freshness. If we happen to be following a systematic, day-by-day Bible reading guide, we might even feel as if God has purposely ordered today's chapters to fall in this order so we could receive those very verses today!

Second, *there was a need to gather up that fresh supply of nour-*

165

ishment "every morning" (Exod. 16:4). A healthy habit of daily "feasting" in God's Word requires discipline. It doesn't happen by accident. The children of Israel had to get up early and go out into the fields to gather up that day's supply of manna. To pray effectively in Jesus' name we need to pursue a daily encounter in God's Word. Each king in ancient Israel was required to keep a copy of God's law close to him so he could "read it all the days of his life, that he may learn to fear the Lord his God . . . that he may prolong his days . . . he and his children . . . " (Deut. 17:19-20). Beloved, days spent without God's Word are weak indeed!

Finally, *each day required a new supply of divine nourishment* (Exod. 16:16-21). Israel quickly discovered God's principle of spiritual spoilage. Moses told them, "No one is to keep any of it until morning" (Exod. 16:19, NIV). This is God's way of telling us we can't live today on yesterday's nourishment. As the psalmist said, "In the morning, O Lord, You hear my voice; in the morning I lay my requests before You" (Ps. 5:3, NIV). David made prayer a daily experience. Little wonder God called him "a man after My own heart!" (Acts 13:22).

So, beloved, tackle today in Jesus' name, the Bread of Life, knowing you've been nourished at His table. Prayerfully declare that He is your Savior, Sustainer, and Supplier in every area where you might feel deficient. Above all, make it a matter of daily spiritual discipline to nourish yourself alone with Jesus, in His Word, before facing the demands of another new day.

TODAY'S PRAYER

I am learning, Father,
that the bread of life does not manifest
in any place where the grain-unto-death
has not been buried.
Today, as I pray in the name of Jesus,
Your gift of the Bread of Life,
I am reminded of the cost expended that
I might be nourished by saving Bread.
"Except a grain of wheat fall into the ground and die . . . "

Now, as I praise Him for His saving death and redeeming life,
I ask that the same might be mirrored in me as
I learn to live and pray in His name.

Help me.
Teach me.
Show me how to die to selfishness
and to any residue of my own way;
that in dying I might be milled in the processes
of Your work in me
and live to become a nourisher of people
my Lord Jesus wants me to touch . . .
in His name.
Amen.

HALLOWING THIS NAME

Bread of God—John 6:33
Bread of Life—John 6:35
Christ Our Life—Col. 3:4
God of My Life—Ps. 42:8
Grain Offering—Lev. 2:1-10
Grain of Wheat—John 12:24
He Who Lives—Rev. 1:18
Hidden Manna—Rev. 2:17
Living Bread—John 6:51
Manna—Exod. 16:31
Portion—Pss. 73:26; 119:57
Portion of My Inheritance—Ps. 16:5
Prince of Life—Acts 3:15
Resurrection and the Life—John 11:25
Strength of My Life—Ps. 27:1
True Bread from Heaven—John 6:32
Way, the Truth, and the Life—John 14:6

29
THE BRIGHT AND MORNING STAR
Revelation 22:16

AWAKENING

In *Nine Lectures on Religions,* Count Nikolaus von Zinzendorf, founder of the Moravian missionary movement in 1727, wrote, "No man can create faith in himself. Something must happen to him which Luther calls 'the divine work in us' which changes us, gives us new birth, and makes us completely different people in heart, spirit, mind, and all our powers."[1]

Zinzendorf was describing a personal spiritual awakening— something that comes to the heart of every individual who has met Jesus Christ as Savior.

Interestingly, it was in a small gathering in 1738 begun by some Moravian missionaries commissioned by Zinzendorf that a young Englishman (who would later impact the world with his revolutionary theology and dynamic preaching) experienced his own spiritual awakening. That Englishman was John Wesley. Of his new-birth experience, Wesley would later write, "I went very unwillingly to a society in Aldersgate Street, where one was reading Luther's preface to the Epistle to the Romans. While he was describing the change which God makes in the heart through faith in Christ, I felt my heart strangely warmed. I felt I did trust in Christ, Christ alone for salvation; and an assurance was given me that He had taken away my sins, even mine, and saved me from the law of sin and death."[2]

John Wesley had met the Bright and Morning Star (Rev. 22:16), the originator of all true spiritual awakening and the divine herald of a genuine "new age!"

KNOWING THIS NAME

There are several words in the Greek language which combine to bring us the concept of Christ as the Bright and Morning Star—the star that heralds the dawning of a new day (Rev. 22:16).

First, *aster,* the Greek word for star used in Revelation 22:16, is combined with the adjectives *bright* and *morning. Bright* indicates Christ's dominance, and *morning* his newness or freshness. The idea here is that Jesus, like the morning star heralding the dawn, outshines the darkness and calls us to be expectant and refreshed.

Second, the Greek word *phosphoros,* from which we derive our word for the element phosphorus, is the word translated "day star," yet another title of Christ found in 2 Peter 1:19 (KJV). It means "light-bearing," and was usually applied to the planet Venus, which often appears with unusual brightness on the eastern horizon just before dawn.

The fact that a related Greek word *phosphorion* (which is translated "window") is derived from the same root word translated as "star" helps us capture the full sense of Christ as our Bright and Morning Star. Jesus brings light in the same way that a window opens a room to the outside sunlight, which then illuminates the entire room. And just as the rising sun (a star in its own right) fills a room with illumination to begin a new day, so Jesus is the Window of God, opening to us all of God's glowing freshness.

A third word, *anatole,* occurs in Luke 1:78. It is translated "Dayspring from on high" in the King James Version and "Sunrise" in newer translations (see the NASB). Interestingly, this same idea of something "rising" is seen in the concept of the Old Testament word *root,* which likewise is mentioned in Revelation 22:16, where Christ is pictured as the Root of David. Just as the sun rises at dawn, so the root shoots up at an early stage.

As a whole, when Jesus refers to himself as the Bright and Morning Star, He is providing us with a threefold analysis of His nature: first, His brightness evidences that the darkness of our sin or suffering cannot prevail; second, His shining declares that a new day is at hand as we move into His light; third, His radiance announces that His coming is at hand—we must look for Him in readiness for He will come again.

All of these insights come in a context that concludes the whole of Scripture. These words of Christ declaring Himself to be the Bright and Morning Star picture how much He longs for us to keep our love for Him fresh as we anticipate His coming.

LIVING THIS NAME

A missionary to Africa described a unique tribal custom that he discovered when going on a prolonged march with natives while serving in the interior. As the tribesmen would retire for the night, just before lying down to sleep, they would say to one another, *"Lutanda, lutanda."* This was their word for "morning star." Speaking it before sleep was a reminder that, by agreement, they would be up and on their way before sunrise. The morning star's appearance would be their signal that dawn was coming soon and it was time to awaken.

How appropriate that Jesus' name, our Morning Star, signals to our hearts a need for alertness as we move into our day awakened in the power of Christ's presence. All meaningful activity for the day must begin with our response to Christ, our Bright and Morning Star, and be sustained by that response throughout the day. And at the heart of that response is an attitude of worship.

An Old Testament prophecy of the coming Messiah helps support this. Numbers 24:17 is the first prophetic reference in the Bible to the promised One (the Messiah) as being a "star." Many scholars believe it was the spread of this prophecy throughout the ancient world that prompted the Persian kings from the East to follow the nativity star to the place where Jesus lay. In a sense, these kings were the first to "awaken" to the Morning Star, to rise up and move into a position of worship before Him (Matt. 2:1-2).

In a practical sense we might say that living in Jesus' name, the Bright and Morning Star, is to rise up and take a spirit of worship into our day. Peter told us we are a "chosen generation, a royal priesthood" appointed to the task of proclaiming "the praises of Him who called [us] out of darkness into His marvelous light" (1 Pet. 2:9). Praise was never intended to be confined to the prayer closet. We are to demonstrate God's praises wherever we go.

And this does not mean so much that we speak or shout our praises all day long as that we reflect God's nature and character in all we do. We are to take His light into the darkness we encounter, whether on the job, in school, or throughout our neighborhood. Jesus said, "You are the light of the world" (Matt 5:14). Significantly, in both 2 Peter 1:19 and Luke 1:78-79, the Morning Star (or Day Star) shines into murky conditions, "a dark place" occupied by those who "sit in darkness" and in "the shadow of death."

Wherever we go in the course of the day, two realities will be inescapable: we are surrounded by people who "sit in darkness," and everywhere we look we will see something of "the shadow of death." To live in Jesus' name is to take the Bright and Morning Star into each of these dark and shadowy circumstances and flood them with Christ's enlightening and awakening power.

PRAYING THIS NAME

"Early will I seek You" is a theme frequently repeated in Scripture (Ps. 63:1; Ps. 57:8, and Ps. 108:2). The phrase literally means, "From the very dawning of the day I will hunger after You." Even Jesus, who prayed "a long while before daylight," saw the value of early communion with His heavenly Father (Mark 1:35).

In a very practical sense, we could begin praying in Jesus' name, the Bright and Morning Star ("He Who Heralds the Morning"), with a commitment to spend time with Christ early in the morning. What better way could we find to awaken our spiritual sensibilities than to immerse ourselves at the start of our day in the fullness of God? Describing such an awakening, D. H. Lawrence wrote in *Shadows*, "And if tonight my soul may find her peace in sleep, and sink in good oblivion, and in the morning wake like a new-opened flower, then I have been dipped again in God, and new-created."[3]

What a way to begin a day, by being "dipped in God" through a prayer encounter in Jesus' name! Oh, that we would heed Paul's "wake up call": "Awake, you who sleep, arise . . . and Christ will give you light!" (Eph. 5:14). Awaken to the bright beams of God's glory shining through His window on eternity! Awaken to the bright hope of a new day in the radiance of His presence. Awaken to this bright reminder: Jesus is coming again! Let these thoughts fill your prayers today in Jesus' name, the Bright and Morning Star.

And as you awaken in His presence, remember that nothing contributes more to powerful prayer for personal awakening than intelligent praise. William Temple in *The Hope of a New World* linked worship with awakening when he wrote, "To worship is to quicken our conscience by the holiness of God, to feed our mind with the truth of God, to purge our imagination by the beauty of God, to open our heart to the love of God, to devote our will to the purpose of God."⁴ Worship, beloved, awakens within us an awareness of the wealth of God available to us today in Jesus' name, our Bright and Morning Star.

TODAY'S PRAYER

Father of Light,
in whom is no change or shadow or turning,
I come in prayer to You.

I want to live as a child of light—
to put off all the hidden works of darkness.
I want to be a light for You wherever I go.
And so I come this day in Jesus' name,
the Bright and Morning Star—
He who heralds the dawn of Your ultimate new day.
May His life in me shine for a glory in this,
another new day of mine.

Today let me so shine that people will see
Your love and life in me
and know that however dark it seems,
You are still around.

Today let my focus be so fixed on Jesus
as the pole star of my living,
that I navigate every turn
as one who lives in the light and not in the night.

Today, I rise to praise You, Lord Jesus.
Come soon.
Come soon, and let the present trumpet-call
announcement of Your Morning Star
become the final symphony of Your ultimate rising as
the Sun of Righteousness to rule over all this earth.

I love You, Lord.
In Your name.
Amen.

HALLOWING THIS NAME

Brightness of His Glory—Heb. 1:3
Chief among Ten Thousand—Song of Sol. 5:10
Day Star—2 Pet. 1:19 (KJV)
Dayspring from On High—Luke 1:78
Forerunner—Heb. 6:20
Light of Israel—Isa. 10:17
Light of the Morning—2 Sam. 23:4
Morning Star—Rev. 2:28
Morning without Clouds—2 Sam. 23:4
Root of David—Rev. 22:16
Star out of Jacob—Num. 24:17
Sun and Shield—Ps. 84:11
Tender Grass—2 Sam. 23:4
Word of God—Rev. 19:13

30
THE WORD OF GOD
Revelation 19:13

CREATIVITY

Samuel Taylor Coleridge, who wrote *On the Prometheus of Aeschylus*, said, "The Hebrew wisdom imperatively asserts an unbeginning creative One who neither became the world, nor is the world eternally, nor made the world out of Himself by emanation or evolution—but willed it, and it was!"[1]

When God willed creation with a word, that Word was actually a person: Jesus Christ. And what a "Word" it was—and is! (See John 1:1 and Colossians 1:12-16.)

To capture a glimpse of the creative power of that Word, let's take an imaginary trip across our universe. Our space vehicle will travel fast—at the speed of light, 186 thousand miles per second. How fast is this? To begin with, we will pass the moon in just 1.3 seconds after blast-off. Traveling at 660 million miles per hour we leave our solar system, that's our sun and its planets, in only five hours.

Four years will then pass before we reach earth's nearest star. While in our galaxy (the Milky Way) we arrive at a new star approximately every five years. In the Milky Way there are at least 100 billion stars; possibly double or triple that number. It's going to be a long journey! If we travel directly across our galaxy in a straight line from earth, it will require eighty thousand years of continuous travel. (If we were to visit every individual star in the Milky Way, 500 billion years would elapse.)

174

Now the trip really begins. Once out of our galaxy it requires 2 million years just to reach our closest neighboring galaxy, Andromeda. Galaxies come in groups, and our group contains approximately seventeen separate galaxies, each with at least 100 billion stars. Some groups have as few as three galaxies. Our group, incidentally, is called by astronomers (without a chuckle) "the Local Group." The largest of the groups in known space is Hercules, which contains ten thousand separate galaxies. We will reach the first of Hercules' galaxies after traveling 300 million years. When our trip is completed, scientists say, we will have passed some hundred octillion—100,000,000,000,000,000,000, 000,000,000—stars. Oh, what a "Word" it was that spoke all of this into being!

KNOWING THIS NAME

It is in John's Revelation that we are introduced to Christ, the Word of God (Rev. 19:13). John's observation is especially significant because this single chapter (Rev. 19) highlights no less than ten names used to describe our Lord, in addition to the name Jesus. Christ is called "the Lord our God" (v. 1); "the Lord God Omnipotent" (v. 6); "the Lamb" (vv. 7, 9); "Faithful" (v. 11); "True" (v. 11); "the Word of God" (v. 13); "Almighty God" (v. 15); "King of Kings" (v. 16); "Lord of Lords" (v. 16); and "the Great God" (v. 17).

But central among all these expressions is the title "the Word of God," the "Word" being God's expression of all He is, a declaration of all of His will and works.

The most graphic expression of this name for Jesus is seen at its introduction in John 1:1. We read, "In the beginning was the Word"! The majestic passage that follows (verses 1-18) incorporates direct references to Jesus as being equal and one with the Father (v. 1); the creator of all things (v. 3); the unquenchable light (v. 5); manifest in the flesh to mankind (v. 14); and the expression of the Father's very heart (v. 17).

Christ's function as Creator, however, is most in evidence when we refer to Him as the Word. He not only made all things but He is able even now to make anything! In his commentary, F. L. Godet wrote, "Eight times in the Genesis narrative of Creation there occurs, like the refrain of a hymn, the words, 'And God said.' John gathers up all those sayings of God into a single saying, living and endowed with activity and intelligence, from which all divine orders emanate; he finds as the basis of all spoken words the Speaking Word."[2]

John said simply, "All things were made through Him, and without Him nothing was made that was made" (John 1:3). The enormity of the significance of these words is that the one who dwells within us by the Holy Spirit is the One who is able to bring worlds into existence with the very breath of His Word. This is the fountainhead of our understanding as to why God's Word upon our lips is so important. When we pray "in God's promises"—when we speak what God's Word says, declaring its truth and its resulting hope into a particular circumstance—there is a creative potential present. This does not mean that we claim this creative power comes from any of us. Rather, we acknowledge the almightiness of God in the person of Christ, the Word of God, who dwells within us and breathes into existence, by His breath, everything that exists.

LIVING THIS NAME

Although Christ longs to breathe His creative power into our day it must be understood that He often chooses to work His creating through us, His creatures. God is the author of music, but He endows men with the capacity to compose and perform it. In *William Shakespeare* Victor Hugo wrote, "God creates art by man having for a tool the human intellect. The Great Workman has made this tool for Himself; He has no other."[3]

Today, for example, we can create a climate of love wherever we go by allowing God to use us to carry His creative Word of love to those in need. Likewise we can bring a creative word of joy to those held captive by fear and despair. To take Jesus' name into our day is to take the "Living Word," Christ Himself, to "him who is weary"! (Isa. 50:4).

And not only does this Word create, it sustains what it has created. Scripture says that Christ is the One "upholding all things by the word of His power" (Heb. 1:3), and that it is in Christ that "all things consist" (Col. 1:17) or are held together. In other words, what Christ has called into being He is able to maintain. And although New Testament Scripture does tell us the heavens and the earth ultimately will pass away (2 Pet. 3:10-12), and that "new heavens and a new earth" will be created (2 Pet. 3:13), it is a fact that creation still exists in its present state because Christ has not withdrawn His creative Word (Ps. 148:6).

Think of it! Everything God has created in the material realm will finally become extinct. Everything, that is, but His Word. It shall "by no means pass away" (Matt. 24:35; Isa. 40:8). As Peter further reminds us, "Now this is the word which by the gospel was preached to you" (1 Pet. 1:25). Hallelujah! Because I have been born into a new creation in Christ (2 Cor. 5:17), my salvation is secure in the Word of God, Christ Himself, and will survive the passing of all creation.

PRAYING THIS NAME

It is clear by our text (Rev. 19:13) that Christ, the Word of God, is the Father's agent riding forth in judgment, His sword (His word) flowing from His mouth, striking down all evil that hinders the establishment of His eternal kingdom (Rev. 19:11-16). This suggests that the Word of God is the expression of Christ's character and ability sent by God to break the forces of hell that would resist His purposes in us. This has thrilling implications for those who would pray today in Jesus' name, the Word of God. For in Christ we have a Savior who creates, sustains, and triumphs.

In Jesus' name we can pray for Christ's creative power to flow into every situation we encounter. His name truly creates. Creativity is defined as "the combining of two separate ideas to form a totally new idea." Therefore, when we pray in Jesus' name and present our ideas to Christ, He combines them with His creative genius, which results in the birth of altogether new ideas. It all can begin with the simplest of prayers, not unlike that of Amy Carmichael:

> Holy Spirit
> think through me
> till Your ideas
> are my ideas.[4]

Also, remember the sustaining power of Jesus' as you pray today; what Christ has created through your previous prayers of faith He is able to maintain. You may have spoken health into a situation that for a time improved but now seems to be weakening. In Jesus' name speak His power to sustain what you have claimed earlier in faith.

177

Beyond all this, don't hesitate to "shout" periodically with a voice of triumph (Ps. 47:1) as you realize that in Jesus' name there is a guarantee of ultimate victory. Jesus not only creates and sustains, He triumphs—and that's worth at least a modest shout. If you think that shouting is an emotional excess strictly reserved for spiritual fanatics, remember this: the same psalmist who challenged us to "rejoice," "praise," "worship," and "pray" commanded us to "shout" (Pss. 5:11; 32:11; 35:27; 132:9).

So why not prayerfully seek out a secluded place where you can lift your voice in unhindered triumph over those potentially troubled prospects of the day. Joyfully exalt Christ, the Word of God, who creates, sustains, and triumphs through His children.

TODAY'S PRAYER

Dear Savior,
I'm glad I know You as the Word.
Just knowing—
knowing that the One who made all worlds,
who was there before anything was,
is overseeing my life—
gives me great confidence to step forth today into
the uncertainties and the requirements of daily duty.

Lord Jesus,
speak into my life today, I pray.
Speak creative thoughts.
Beget creative events.
Flow creative life.
Let words of Your invention flow through me to heal people.
Let ideas of Your origin course through me to serve others.
Let newness of life in You influence hope wherever I go,
that a world of people
who are by-and-large without it
might look up . . .
and see You.

And one more thing, Lord.
Thank You that the Word, which You are incarnately,
has been given to me in precious promises,
written for my reading and receiving.
I ask You, Jesus, let each promise I need for today

become life—practical reality—in me.
Because You are the Word and dwell in me,
make its fullness overflow through me.
Reveal Your Word, I pray.
In Jesus' name.
Amen.

HALLOWING THIS NAME

Beginning—Col. 1:18
Beginning of the Creation of God—Rev. 3:14
Creator of All Things—Col. 1:16
Creator of the Ends of the Earth—Isa. 40:28
Emmanuel (God with Us)—Matt. 1:23
Faithful Witness—Rev. 1:5
Forerunner—Heb. 6:20
Image of God—2 Cor. 4:4
Jehovah-Elohim (The Eternal Creator)—Gen. 2:4-25
Jehovah-Hosenu (The Lord Our Maker)—Ps. 95:6
Lord Who Created the Heavens—Isa. 45:18
Maker of All Things—Jer. 51:19
My Maker—Job 35:10
Witness to the People—Isa. 55:4
Word—John 1:1
Word of Life—1 John 1:1
Your Maker—Isa. 54:5

31
THE CAPTAIN OF THE HOST
OF THE LORD
Joshua 5:14

VICTORY

Massena, one of Napoleon's generals during his reign in France, suddenly appeared before an undefended Austrian town with a regiment of eighteen thousand troops. The town council was just about to surrender when the elderly minister of the community church reminded them it was Easter. He begged them to hold services as usual, trusting the Lord to handle the trouble. Reluctantly, the council agreed. Amazingly, upon hearing the church bells ringing joyfully, the French regiment concluded that the entire Austrian army had come to the town's defense, and they fled in terror. An army of eighteen thousand had been beaten by a bell.

Victories for God's people come in all shapes and sizes. Sometimes it even seems that God sets up certain situations to show His sovereignty. From His vantage point the view is always victory. As Puritan revivalist Jonathan Edwards explained in *A History of the Work of Redemption*:

> God, doubtless, is pursuing some design and carrying on some scheme in the various changes and revolutions which from age to age come to pass in the world. It is most reasonable to suppose that all revolutions, from the beginning of the world to the end of it, are but the various parts

of the same scheme, all conspiring to bring to pass that great event which the Great Creator and Governor of the World has ultimately in view.[1]

KNOWING THIS NAME

God's ultimate view of victory is summed up in a person: the Lord Jesus Christ. And in our journey to a better understanding of what it means to live and pray in Jesus' name we come to our final title for consideration: The Captain of the Host of the Lord (Josh. 5:14, KJV).

The biblical setting for this title occurs just after Israel's crossing of the Jordan and immediately prior to the battle of Jericho. Joshua was apparently off checking into the challenging prospect of attacking this well-fortified city when the Lord appeared to him (Josh. 5:13-15). This encounter reveals the Lord as Captain of the Host of the Lord (or "Commander of the Army of the Lord," NIV). Also, in the first five verses of chapter six, God issued Joshua a list of rather strange steps for his people to take if they wished to see a victory at Jericho (see Josh. 6:1-5).

The fact that Christ Himself appears to Joshua in this setting is called by theologians a "Christophany," from the Greek words *Christos* meaning Christ, and *phaneros,* meaning manifestation. "Christophanies" are appearances or manifestations of Christ prior to His birth. (Other such manifestations include the Lord's physical appearance to Abraham in Genesis 18 and His appearance to Samson's parents in Judges 13:20.)

The Jericho appearance of Christ is noteworthy because of His rather unusual response to Joshua's question, "Are You for us or for our enemies?" (Joshua 5:13, NIV). Christ answers, "Neither . . . but as commander of the army of the Lord I have now come" (v. 14, NIV). In other words, Christ is saying only that He has come into the conflict to work the will of God. The thought here is this: "I'm here to do what the Father desires, not what any man has determined by his own limited reasoning to be best in this situation."

The victories the Lord wants to give us require that we be both committed and submitted to His plans and purposes, rather than persuaded by our own opinions or interests. When Abraham Lincoln was asked during the Civil War if he believed God was on his side, he answered, "I'm not so concerned as to whether or not

God is on my side as I am concerned to know if I am on His!"

Jesus Himself serves as a beautiful example of this spirit of submission in Hebrews: "For it was fitting for Him, for whom are all things and by whom are all things, in bringing many sons to glory, to make the author [the Greek *archegos*, meaning 'leader or captain'] of their salvation perfect [complete] through sufferings" (Heb. 2:10).

The point here is that the pathway to victory often goes through a valley of sorrow or suffering. But we have this unshakable hope: no matter the scope of the conflict or the degree of the suffering, our Captain is present—and He has been here before. Jesus knows precisely what to do!

LIVING THIS NAME

There are, in a sense, two titles in this one phrase, "the Captain of the Host of the Lord." Christ is our Captain in conflict as well as the Lord of Hosts in our warfare. This provides tremendous encouragement as we face today's battles in Jesus' name. The armies of heaven, innumerable angels by earth's accounting, are at Christ's command. And He now directs those hosts—which He chose not to summon for His own rescue at Calvary—to serve our interests (Matt. 26:53; Heb. 1:14).

The New Testament equivalent of the Old Testament title "Lord of Hosts" is Jehovah-Sabaoth (Rom. 9:29; James 5:4). In explaining this New Testament title Charles Spurgeon said, "The Lord (Jehovah-Sabaoth) rules the angels, the stars, the elements, and all the hosts of heaven and the heaven of heavens is under His sway. The armies of men, though they know it not, are made to subserve His will. As the General of the forces of the land, the Lord High Admiral of the seas, Christ is on our side—our supreme ally; woe unto those who fight against Him, for they shall flee like smoke before the wind when He gives the word to scatter them."[2]

In Isaiah 37:36 the prophet Isaiah gives a remarkable example of this angelic power. Here, a lone angel at the direction of the Lord of Hosts destroys a vast army of almost two-hundred thousand Assyrians in a single night. Think of it! If just one angel can do this much damage, imagine the potential of the twelve legions of angels (a total of seventy-two thousand angels) that Jesus said He could have released at His crucifixion had He so desired

(Matt. 26:53). Then consider the thrilling fact that these heavenly messengers are now at our disposal (Heb. 1:14). Little wonder Luther could write:

> Did we in our own strength confide,
> Our striving would be losing,
> Were not the right Man on our side,
> The Man of God's own choosing.
> Dost ask who that may be?
> Christ Jesus, it is He;
> Lord Sabaoth His name,
> From age to age the same,
> And He must win the battle.[3]

PRAYING THIS NAME

Practical lessons for personal prayer abound in Joshua's Jericho encounter with Christ, his Captain (Josh. 5:13–6:6). And these lessons are valuable to us for living and praying effectively in the name of our Lord and Captain.

First, *never enter a battle without consulting the Captain!* The victory God wants us to experience today in Jesus' name requires that we receive our Captain's strategy for battle. Like Joshua, we need a face-to-face encounter with Christ in personal prayer. We shouldn't expect God to speak to us if we're not available to listen.

Second, *worship the Lord in reverence and humility before seeking His guidance!* Joshua fell on his face humbly before God as an act of worship and reverence before he asked, "What message does my Lord have for His servant?" (Josh. 5:14, NIV). True, we have often emphasized worship in our study—but it can never be emphasized enough!

Third, *pursue patterns of personal purity as the result of encountering Christ!* If we listen carefully during our times of quiet intimacy with the Lord, we'll surely hear Him say as He did to Joshua, "Take off your sandals, for the place where you are standing is holy" (Joshua 5:15, NIV). Purity is essential to productive praying. Scripture reminds us that it is the prayer of a "righteous" person that avails much (James 5:16).

Fourth, *only those who listen and obey will experience the totality of Christ's promised victory!* Joshua not only listened to what his

Captain said, he obeyed Him in every detail. Obedience is the key to victory. Nothing delights or honors God more than an obedient spirit.

In his imaginative work *The Screwtape Letters*, C. S. Lewis pictures a senior demon in the echelons of hellish hierarchy, whom he names Screwtape, giving instructions to his nephew, Wormwood, a junior demon just learning the tricks of the trade. Screwtape repeatedly warns Wormwood to be on guard for signs that he is losing his "patient" to the control of the "Enemy" (Screwtape's term for God).

At one point Screwtape addresses his nephew on the issue of obedience. He cautions, "Do not be deceived, Wormwood. Our cause is never more in danger than when a human, no longer desiring, but still intending, to do our Enemy's will looks round upon a universe from which every trace of Him seems to have vanished, and asks why he has been forsaken, and still obeys."[4]

Beloved, Christ is our Captain and His promise of victory is available today to those who not only listen, but obey in Jesus' name! Scripture clearly links obedience with answered prayer. John wrote: "We receive from Him whatever we ask for, because we (watchfully) obey His orders—observe His suggestions and injunctions, follow His plan for us—and (habitually) practice what is pleasing to Him" (1 John 3:22, Amp).

So let's go forth courageously today to conquer in the name of Jesus. Nothing we could ever need—strength, growth, joy, provision, purpose, peace—escapes the power of Christ's person. Describe a desire or voice a virtue, and you will find its complete fulfillment in Jesus' name. That's why we can pray so freely with St. Francis of Assisi:

> You are holy, Lord, the only God, and Your deeds
>   are wonderful.
> You are strong, You are great.
> You are the most high,
> You are almighty.
> You, holy Father, are King of heaven and earth.
> You are Three and One, Lord God, all good.
> You are good, all good, supreme good, Lord God,
>   living and true.
> You are love, You are wisdom.

You are humility, You are endurance.
You are rest, You are peace.
You are joy and gladness, You are justice and moderation.
You are riches, and You suffice for us.
You are beauty, You are gentleness.
You are protector, You are our guardian and defender.
You are courage, You are our heaven and our hope.
You are our faith, our great consolation.
You are our eternal life, great and wonderful
Lord, God Almighty, Merciful Savior.[5]

TODAY'S PRAYER

A Poem of Praise

I saw the King last night.
He was reentering the gates;
But the scene somehow was different than before.
There were praising hosts and children singing out loud hosannas there,
As He passed triumphant through Jerusalem's door.
But their hands did not hold branches,
And their coats were not cast down,
And the King did not a lowly colt employ.
But the greeters each held trumpets,
And their glistening garments wore
And their praise suffused His entry with their joy.
The King was on a stallion white, a mighty prancing steed,
And a glorious air the greeters' voices raised:
"Hail the Conquering One, King Jesus,
who has gone forth conquering—
King of Glory, enter now these gates called Praise."

Then I knew it was a vision—now repeated every time
Open hearts prepare His way with worshiping.
Just as long ago He entered; Just as some day He'll return,
So today He waits to enter as we sing.
Now He comes to reign in glory, nevermore to leave again
As ensued upon His first triumphal day;
When He entered He was cast out to Golgotha's scene of death,
And the demon hordes presumed they'd won their way.
But He rose—He shook the shackles from His nail-pierced hands and feet.

Now with hands of holy power bears His sword;
And He marches to the battle—slaying evil, searing hell—
As the Captain of the hosts of God—the Lord!

He has come to dwell among us, ne'er again to know defeat,
And we lift our voices boldly to the skies.
To our lips we place the trumpets, silver praises loudly sung,
"Hail, all hail to Jesus, Lord of Paradise!"

Can you read this vision glorious? Can you understand my dream
which the revelation picture helps me tell?
One upon a white horse conquering, going forth again, again
Daily warring over darkest hosts of hell.
"He went conq'ring and to conquer," John the seer saw the scene.
And he prophesied the conflict of our day;

How the King who seemed defeated after His triumphal entry,
Now through Calvary's vict'ry comes again to stay.
He abides and makes His dwelling where pure hearts sustain His praise;
He reenters to their glad triumphal song.
He will gird Himself for battle and go forth—again, again—
Forth to conquer sin and evil, just as long . . .
Just as long as wise hearts worship, just as long as some still know
That the battle is not ours, it is the Lord's.

And as praise goes forth, so He does; and new victories secures,
And new triumph scenes become our great reward.
So lift ceaseless praise, redeemed ones, singing, "Worthy is the Lamb,
Who as Judah's Lion roars upon His prey,"
His the battle, ours the worship;
His the triumph, ours the song.
His reentry ours to sing at every day.

J.W.H.

HALLOWING THIS NAME

Author of Faith—Heb. 12:2
Captain of Our Salvation—Heb. 2:10 (KJV)
Commander—Isa. 55:4
Deliverer—Rom. 11:26
Great God—Titus 2:13

He Who Is Coming—Heb. 10:36-37
He Who Shall Have Dominion—Num. 24:19
Jehovah-Nissi (The Lord Our Banner)—Exod. 17:15
Jehovah-Sabaoth (The Lord of Hosts)—1 Sam. 1:3; Isa. 6:3
Leader—Isa. 55:4
Lion of the Tribe of Judah—Rev. 5:5
Lord God of Hosts—Ps. 59:5
Lord Mighty in Battle—Ps. 24:8
Lord Strong and Mighty—Ps. 24:8
Man of War—Exod. 15:3
Mighty One—Ps. 45:3
Resurrection—John 11:25
Rod from the Stem of Jesse—Isa. 11:1
Shield—2 Sam. 22:31
Sword of Your Majesty—Deut. 33:29

NOTES

Introduction
1. Andrew Murray, *With Christ in the School of Prayer,* rev. ed. (Springdale, Penn.: Whitaker House, 1987), 174.

Chapter 1
1. Veronica Zundel, *Eerdmans' Book of Famous Prayers* (Grand Rapids: Eerdmans, 1983), 33.

Chapter 2
1. Zundel, *Famous Prayers,* 33.
2. Ibid., 64.

Chapter 3
1. David Manning White, *The Search for God* (New York: Macmillan, 1983), 25.
2. Ibid., 305.
3. Zundel, *Famous Prayers,* 78.
4. Ibid., 18.

Chapter 4
1. Zundel, *Famous Prayers,* 70.

Chapter 5
1. White, *The Search for God,* 133.
2. Ibid., 20.
3. Ibid., 135.
4. Zundel, *Famous Prayers,* 90.

Chapter 7
1. White, *The Search for God,* 11.
2. Ibid., 327.
3. Zundel, *Famous Prayers,* 81.

Chapter 8
1. White, *The Search for God,* 46.
2. Ibid., 115.
3. Zundel, *Famous Prayers,* 51.
4. Ibid., 51.

Chapter 9
1. White, *The Search for God,* 309.
2. Ibid., 308.
3. Ibid., 29.
4. Ibid., 305.
5. Ibid., 19.
6. Ibid., 270.
7. Zundel, *Famous Prayers,* 78.

Chapter 10
1. White, *The Search for God,* 165.
2. Ibid., 54.

Chapter 11
1. White, *The Search for God,* 10.
2. Ibid., 264.

Chapter 12
1. White, *The Search for God,* 268.
2. Ibid., 40.
3. Ibid., 50.
4. Zundel, *Famous Prayers,* 62.

Chapter 13
1. White, *The Search for God,* 195.
2. Zundel, *Famous Prayers,* 49.

Chapter 14
1. Lecture notes from Change the World School of Prayer, Change the World
   Ministries, P.O. Box 5838, Mission Hills, CA 91345.
2. White, *The Search for God,* 31.

Chapter 15
1. White, *The Search for God,* 139.

Chapter 16
1. White, *The Search for God,* 9.
2. Ibid., 47.
3. Zundel, *Famous Prayers,* 35.

Chapter 18
1. White, *The Search for God,* 43.
2. Ibid., 16.
3. Ibid., 13.
4. Herbert Lockyer, *All the Divine Names and Titles in the Bible* (Grand Rapids:
   Zondervan, 1975), 127.
5. Zundel, *Famous Prayers,* 41.

Chapter 19
1. Zundel, *Famous Prayers,* 65.
2. Franz Delitzsch, *Commentaries on the Old Testament,* Vol. VII, 251.

Chapter 20
1. White, *The Search for God,* 27.
2. Ibid., 22.
3. Zundel, *Famous Prayers,* 39.

Chapter 21
1. White, *The Search for God,* 142.
2. Zundel, *Famous Prayers,* 58.
3. White, *The Search for God,* 228.

Chapter 22
1. White, *The Search for God,* 235.
2. Ibid., 13.
3. Lecture notes from Change the World School of Prayer, Change the World Ministries, P.O. Box 5838, Mission Hills, CA 91345.

Chapter 23
1. Zundel, *Famous Prayers,* 22.
2. Ibid., 43.

Chapter 24
1. White, *The Search for God,* 178.
2. Ibid., 288.
3. Ibid., 328.
4. Zundel, *Famous Prayers,* 43.

Chapter 25
1. White, *The Search for God,* 41.
2. Ibid., 39.
3. Lockyer, *Divine Names and Titles,* 264.
4. White, *The Search for God,* 48-49.
5. Zundel, *Famous Prayers,* 113.
6. Ibid., 40.

Chapter 26
1. White, *The Search for God,* 267.
2. William A. Ogden, "He Is Able to Deliver Thee," *Great Hymns of the Faith,* (Grand Rapids: Zondervan Publishing House, 1968), 201.

Chapter 29
1. White, *The Search for God,* 228.
2. John Winnmill Brown, *Every Knee Shall Bow* (Old Tappan, NJ: Fleming H. Revell Company, 1984), 45.
3. White, *The Search for God,* 18.
4. Ibid., 151.

Chapter 30
1. White, *The Search for God,* 10.
2. Lockyer, *Divine Names and Titles,* 271.
3. White, *The Search for God,* 22.
4. Zundel, *Famous Prayers,* 69.

Chapter 31
1. White, *The Search for God*, 60.
2. Lockyer, *Divine Names and Titles*, 43.
3. Martin Luther, "A Mighty Fortress Is Our God," *Great Hymns of the Faith* (Grand Rapids: Zondervan Publishing House, 1968), 36.
4. C. S. Lewis, *The Screwtape Letters* (New York: Macmillan, 1961), 39.
5. Zundel, *Famous Prayers,* 30.

NAMES OF JESUS

Adonai-Jehovah (Sovereign Lord; Master Jehovah)—Gen. 15:2, 8
Advocate—1 John 2:1
All in All—Col. 3:11
Altogether Lovely—Song of Sol. 5:16
Ancient of Days—Dan. 7:13-14
Angel of His Presence—Isa. 63:9
Apostle and High Priest—Heb. 3:1
Apostle of Our Confession—Heb. 3:1
Arm of the Lord—Isa. 51:9-10
As Rivers of Water in a Dry Place—Isa. 32:2
Author of Eternal Salvation—Heb. 5:9
Author of Our Faith—Heb. 12:2

Balm of Gilead—Jer. 8:22
Banner of the Nations—Isa. 11:12
Beginning—Col. 1:18
Beginning of the Creation of God—Rev. 3:14
Bishop of Your Souls—1 Pet. 2:25 (KJV)
Blessed and Only Potentate—1 Tim. 6:15
Branch of Righteousness—Jer. 23:5
Branch out of His Roots—Isa. 11:1
Branch of the Lord—Isa. 4:2
Bread of God—John 6:33
Bread of Life—John 6:35

Firstfruits of Those Who Have Fallen Asleep—1 Cor. 15:20
Flame—Isa. 10:17
Forerunner—Heb. 6:20
Foundation—Isa. 28:16
Fountain of Living Waters—Jer. 17:13-14
Friend Who Sticks Closer than a Brother—Prov. 18:24

Garden of Renown—Ezek. 34:29
Gift of God—John 4:10
Glorious Lord—Isa. 33:21 (KJV)
Glorious Throne to His Father's House—Isa. 22:23
Glory of Your People Israel—Luke 2:32
God Full of Compassion—Ps. 86:15
God Manifest in the Flesh—1 Tim. 3:16
God My Savior—Luke 1:47
God of All Comfort—2 Cor. 1:3
God of All Grace—1 Pet. 5:10
God of Glory—Acts 7:2
God of Hope—Rom. 15:13
God of Love and Peace—2 Cor. 13:11
God of My Life—Ps. 42:8
God of Patience and Comfort—Rom. 15:5
God of Peace—Rom. 15:33
God of Recompense—Jer. 51:56
God of the Whole Earth—Isa. 54:5
God of Truth—Deut. 32:4
God the Judge of All—Heb. 12:23
Good—Ps. 34:8
Good Shepherd—John 10:11
Good Teacher—Mark 10:17
Governor—Matt. 2:6 (KJV)
Grain Offering—Lev. 2:1-10
Grain of Wheat—John 12:23-24
Great High Priest—Heb. 4:14
Great King above All Gods—Ps. 95:3
Great Light—Isa. 9:2
Great Prophet—Luke 7:16
Great Shepherd of the Sheep—Heb. 13:20

Habitation of Justice—Jer. 50:7
He Who Fills All in All—Eph. 1:23
He Who Lives—Rev. 1:18

He Who Will Come—Heb. 10:36-37
Head of Every Man—1 Cor. 11:3
Head of the Body—Col. 1:18
Head Over All Things—Eph. 1:22
Heir of All Things—Heb. 1:2
Help of My Countenance—Ps. 42:11
Hidden Manna—Rev. 2:17
Hiding Place from the Wind—Isa. 32:2
High and Lofty One—Isa. 57:15
Highest—Luke 1:76
His Only Begotten Son—John 3:16
Holy—Isa. 57:15
Holy and Awesome—Ps. 111:9
Holy and True—Rev. 6:10
Holy One and the Just—Acts 3:14
Holy One of Israel—Isa. 29:19; 49:7
Hope of Glory—Col. 1:27
Hope of Israel—Jer. 17:13
Hope of Their Fathers—Jer. 50:7
Horn of Salvation—Luke 1:69

I AM—John 8:58
Image of God—2 Cor. 4:4
Image of the Invisible God—Col. 1:15
Immanuel (God with Us)—Matt. 1:23

Jehovah-Elohay (The Lord My God)—Zech. 14:5
Jehovah-Eloheka (The Lord Your God)—Exod. 20:2
Jehovah-Elohim (The Eternal Creator)—Gen. 2:4-25
Jehovah-Elyon (The Lord Most High)—Ps. 7:17
Jehovah-Hosenu (The Lord Our Maker)—Ps. 95:6
Jehovah-Jireh (The Lord Will Provide)—Gen. 22:8-14
Jehovah-Mekaddishkem (The Lord Our Sanctifier)—Lev. 20:8
Jehovah-Nissi (The Lord My Banner)—Exod. 17:15
Jehovah-Rohi (The Lord My Shepherd)—Ps. 23:1
Jehovah-Ropheka (The Lord Your Healer)—Exod. 15:26
Jehovah-Sabaoth (The Lord of Hosts)—1 Sam. 1:3; Isa. 6:3
Jehovah-Shalom (The Lord Our Peace)—Judg. 6:24
Jehovah-Shammah (The Lord Is There)—Ezek. 48:35
Jehovah-Tsidkenu (The Lord Our Righteousness)—Jer. 23:6; 33:16
Jesus Christ the Righteous—1 John 2:1
Judge and Lawgiver—Isa. 33:22

Judge of the Living and the Dead—Acts 10:42
Just One—Acts 7:52

King—Zech. 14:16
King In His Beauty—Isa. 32:17
King of Glory—Ps. 24:10
King of Israel—John 1:49
King of Jacob—Isa. 41:21
King of Kings—Rev. 17:14
King of Peace—Heb. 7:2
King of Righteousness—Heb. 7:2
King of the Saints—Rev. 15:3
King over All the Earth—Zech. 14:9
King's Son—Ps. 72:1

Lamb in the Midst of the Throne—Rev. 7:17
Lamb of God—John 1:29
Lamb Slain—Rev. 5:12
Lamb without Blemish—1 Pet. 1:19
Leader—Isa. 55:4
Life-Giving Spirit—1 Cor. 15:45
Light of Israel—Isa. 10:17
Light of Men—John 1:4
Light of the City—Rev. 21:23
Light to the Gentiles—Isa. 42:6; Luke 2:32
Light of the Morning—2 Sam. 23:4
Light of the World—John 8:12
Lily of the Valleys—Song of Sol. 2:1
Lion of the Tribe of Judah—Rev. 5:5
Living Bread—John 6:51
Living Stone—1 Pet. 2:4
Lord—Rom. 10:13
Lord and Savior Jesus Christ—2 Pet. 3:18
Lord of Both the Dead and the Living—Rom. 14:9
Lord from Heaven—1 Cor. 15:47
Lord God Almighty—Rev. 4:8
Lord God of Truth—Ps. 31:5
Lord God Omnipotent—Rev. 19:6
Lord Mighty in Battle—Ps. 24:8
Lord Most High—Ps. 47:2
Lord of All—Acts 10:36
Lord of All the Earth—Zech. 6:5

Lord of Lords—Rev. 17:14
Lord Our Maker—Ps. 95:6
Lord Our Righteousness—Jer. 23:6
Lord over All—Rom. 10:12
Lord Strong and Mighty—Ps. 24:8
Lord Who Created the Heavens—Isa. 45:18
Lord Your Redeemer—Isa. 43:14
Love—1 John 4:8

Maker—Isa. 17:7
Maker of All Things—Jer. 51:19
Man Attested by God—Acts 2:22
Man of Sorrows—Isa. 53:3
Man of War—Exod. 15:3
Manna—Exod. 16:31
Master of the House—Luke 13:25
Mediator—Job 9:33; 1 Tim. 2:5
Mediator of a Better Covenant—Heb. 8:6
Mediator of the New Covenant—Heb. 12:24
Messenger of the Covenant—Mal. 3:1
Messiah—John 4:25
Mighty God—Isa. 9:6
Mighty One—Ps. 45:3
Mighty One of Israel—Isa. 30:29
Mighty One of Jacob—Isa. 60:16
Minister of the Sanctuary—Heb. 8:2
Morning Star—Rev. 2:28
Morning without Clouds—2 Sam. 23:4
Most High—Ps. 18:13
Most Holy—Dan. 9:24
My Beloved—Matt. 12:18
My Elect One—Isa. 42:1
My Fortress—Ps. 12:2
My Glory—Ps. 3:3
My Help—Ps. 115:11
My Helper—Heb. 13:6
My High Tower—Ps. 144:2
My Hope—Ps. 71:5
My Lamp—2 Sam. 22:29
My Lord and My God—John 20:28
My Maker—Job 35:10

My Portion—Pss. 73:26; 119:57
My Power—2 Sam. 22:33
My Righteous Servant—Isa. 53:11
My Rock of Refuge—Ps. 31:2
My Salvation—Ps. 38:22
My Shepherd—Ps. 23:1
My Shield—2 Sam. 22:3
My Song—Isa. 12:2
My Strength—2 Sam. 22:3
My Strength and My Song—Isa. 12:2
My Support—2 Sam. 22:19; Ps. 18:18
My Well Beloved—Isa. 5:1

O Lord God of Hosts—Ps. 59:5
Offering—Eph. 5:2
Ointment Poured Forth—Song of Sol. 1:3
One I Love—Song of Sol. 3:2
One Shepherd—John 10:16
One Who Shall Have Dominion—Num. 24:19
Only Begotten of the Father—John 1:14
Only Wise God—1 Tim. 1:17 (KJV)
Our Hope—1 Tim. 1:1
Our Great God—Titus 2:13
Our Lawgiver—Isa. 33:22
Our Passover—1 Cor. 5:7
Our Peace—Eph. 2:14
Our Potter—Isa. 64:8

Peace Offering—Lev. 3:1-5
Physician—Luke 4:23
Polished Shaft—Isa. 49:2
Portion of Jacob—Jer. 10:16; 51:19
Portion of My Inheritance—Ps. 16:5
Precious Stone—1 Pet. 2:6
Priest Forever—Heb. 5:6
Prince and Savior—Acts 5:30-31
Prince of Life—Acts 3:15
Prince of Peace—Isa. 9:6
Prince of Princes—Dan. 8:25
Propitiation for Our Sins—1 John 2:2

Rabbi—John 1:49
Rain upon the Mown Grass—Ps. 72:6

Stone—Matt. 21:42
Stone Cut Out without Hands—Dan. 2:34-35
Stone of Israel—Gen. 49:24
Stone of Stumbling—1 Pet. 2:8
Strength of My Life—Ps. 27:1
Strength to the Needy—Isa. 25:4
Strength to the Poor—Isa. 25:4
Strong Lord—Ps. 89:8 (KJV)
Strong Tower—Ps. 61:3
Stronghold—Nahum 1:7
Sun and Shield—Ps. 84:11
Sun of Righteousness—Mal. 4:2
Sure Foundation—Isa. 28:16
Surety—Heb. 7:22
Sword of Your Majesty—Deut. 33:29

Teacher—Matt. 23:8; John 13:13
Tender Grass—2 Sam. 23:4
Testator—Heb. 9:16
That Eternal Life—1 John 1:2
That Spiritual Rock—1 Cor. 10:4
Tower of Salvation—2 Sam. 22:51
Trap and a Snare—Isa. 8:14
Tried Stone—Isa. 28:16
True Bread from Heaven—John 6:32
True God—1 John 5:20
True Light—John 1:9

Understanding—Prov. 8:14
Unspeakable Gift—2 Cor. 9:15 (KJV)
Upholder of All Things—Heb. 1:3

Vine—John 15:5

Way, the Truth, the Life—John 14:6
Wisdom—Prov. 8:12
Wisdom of God—1 Cor. 1:24
Witness to the People—Isa. 55:4
Wonderful—Isa. 9:6
Word—John 1:1
Word of God—Rev. 19:13
Word of Life—1 John 1:1